WALLEYE TROUBLE-SHOOTING

This book has 50 simple, common sense answers to your toughest on-the-water questions. Its practical information is based on my successful tournament experience from walleye waters around the U.S. and Canada.

BY MIKE McCLELLAND

Photography by Fishing Enterprises, unless noted otherwise
Layout and Design by Jim McClelland
Artwork and Illustrations by Leslee McClelland

Walleye Trouble-Shooting

Copyright © 1996 by Fishing Enterprises, Inc.
First Printing February 1996
ISBN: 0-9622571-8-4 (Hardcover);
0-9622571-7-6 (Library binding);
0-9622571-9-2 (Softcover)

All rights reserved. No part of this book may be used or reproduced in any form or by any means, or stored in a database or retrieval system, without written permission by the author, his assigns or heirs. Brief quotations in articles or reviews are permissible, however.

This book is sold as is, without warranty of any kind, either express or implied. Neither the author nor distributors shall be liable with respect to any liability, loss, or damage alleged to be caused directly or indirectly by this book. In other words, don't sue us for anything that might "go wrong" as a result of your reading this book!

Contents

Forward..v
Acknowledgements...vi

Part I - What You Need To Know

1. How Can I Become A Better Fisherman?.....................1
2. What's The Quickest Way To Increase My Catch?.........5
3. What Is The Best Way To Fish My Home Lake?............9
4. Does Color Make A Difference?..................................11
5. Does Fish Scent Make Walleyes Bite?........................15
6. Does Fish Scent Work?...17
7. Does Tournament Fishing Affect The Resource?........19

Part II - What You Need To Buy

8. Do I Need A $25,000 Boat?......................................25
9. Why Is Boat Control Critical?...................................31
10. What Electronics Should I Buy?..............................35
11. Do I Need A GPS?..39
12. How Do You Choose The Right Rod?.......................43
13. Do Long Rods Really Help?....................................49
14. What Kind Of Line Should I Use?...........................55
15. Should I Change To The New Super Lines?............59
16. Why Do You Use Light Line?..................................61
17. What Knots Are For What?....................................65
18. What Size or Color Of Hooks Do I Need?................69
19. What's A Crankbait?..73
20. What's A Bottom Bouncer?....................................77
21. How Do You Choose The Best Live Bait?................81

Part III - Where You Need To Go

22. What's The Fastest Way To Locate Walleyes?...............85
23. How Do You Locate Walleyes In Reservoirs & Lakes?..91
24. What About Current?..97
25. What About Pre-Spawn Walleyes?................................101
26. When & Where Do Walleyes Spawn?............................105
27. How Do I Catch Walleyes After The Spawn?................109
28. What About Fall Walleyes?..117
29. How Do You Find Walleyes In Weeds?.......................121
30. How Do You Find Shallow Water Walleyes?................125
31. How Do You Catch Walleyes After A Cold Front?......131
32. Are There Suspended Walleyes In My Lake?..............135

Part IV - What You Need To Do

33. How Can I Get A Better Hook-Set?............................139
34. How Do You Prevent Short Hits?..............................143
35. What's Your Favorite All-Around Technique?.............149
36. How Do You Know When To Switch Presentations?...151
37. Why Have Crankbaits Become So Popular?................153
38. What's The Most Important Part Of Trolling?...........161
39. When & How Should I Troll?....................................167
40. How Can I Catch More Fish Trolling?.......................171
41. When Should You Use Trolling Boards?.....................175
42. What's The Key To Casting Crankbaits?....................179
43. When Do You Fish A Bottom Bouncer?......................183
44. How Do You Fish Jigs?...187
45. When Do You Fish A Lindy Rig?...............................191
46. When Should I Use Bobbers?....................................195
47. How Do You Fish Current From The Bank?..............199
48. What's The Best Way To Catch Walleyes In Weeds?...203
49. Why Should You Fish The Windy Side?....................209
50. What Do You Do About Too Much Boat Pressure?......215

FORWARD - ABOUT THE AUTHOR

Fishing with Mike McClelland is an experience. For some, it would be an experience in frustration because he does more "looking" than fishing. He's never content with what he's catching; his inner goal is to understand Mother Nature. That drive, coupled with an extraordinary amount of time on the water, and an attitude that says, "I can do it better," has propelled Mike to the top of the walleye pro ranks.

Actually, Mike would be at the top of any profession he elected, and right now he's into tackle manufacturing, book-writing, seminars, Crankbait Depth Guide distribution and product design for the tackle and marine industry. He is a threat to win any time he enters a walleye tournament.

When I first met Mike, he was on a "must-win" basis. He needed to win just to move onto the next tournament. In winter, he kept a grueling seminar schedule in hopes of earning enough money to reach the next. Love of the sport and a desire to excel fueled his inner fires. That was apparent to those of us who were fortunate to know Mike in those early years.

Fishing to Mike is a puzzle. No, fishing to him is developing a *solution* to the puzzle. He uses every wisp of cloud, blip on his electronics and tap on his bottom bouncer to telegraph his brain what's happening. Then, a reaction takes place. That reaction to surrounding conditions and an ability to make both strategic and tactical changes on the water has helped Mike cash many big tournament checks.

Mike's reaction is the reason why so many people, from weekend anglers to industry experts, respect his opinion. When Mike offers recommendations, it is from the perspective of someone who has been there. Throughout the time I've know him, he has been vocal about the issues of the day. He was one of the first to recommend that the PWT go to a Pro-Am format. He was one of the first to successfully fish shallow water for walleyes. He was one of the first winners to describe the intimate detail of his three Team of the Year wins on the MWC trail. He told Mercury engineers exactly what their outboards were doing and what he thought would make them better -- they followed his advice. He worked closely with lure companies; they even have a series of crankbaits with Mike's name on them. The same is true for Mike's rod sponsor and its new walleye rods.

Mike has been loyal to the companies he represents. Honesty and straight-forwardness are two characteristics he conveys at all times. This book addresses walleye the same way and will open another window into this exciting sport for every reader. It's in the usual Mike McClelland mode -- Just the facts.

Jim Kalkofen
Executive Director, In-Fisherman Professional Walleye Trail

ACKNOWLEDGEMENTS

I wish to thank the following, without which this book wouldn't be a reality: Gary Parsons; Keith Kavajecz; Daryl Christensen; Rick LaCourse; Joe Hughes; Jack McClelland; Jim Kalkofen; Steve Nelson; and Jim McClelland.

A special thanks to editor Julie Anderson, she have given this book a professional touch. Her advice and suggestions has made this book well-written and easy to read.

To Bob Propst, Sr., Gary Roach and all of my fishing partners, both professional and amateur, who have helped me to better understand walleyes and walleye fishing.

Part I

WHAT YOU NEED TO KNOW

South Dakota Tourism Photo

HOW DO I BECOME A BETTER FISHERMAN?

This first question could well be the title of this book. Although there are over 50 in-depth answers to your most frequently asked questions, these answers are still just bits and pieces of the huge puzzle of understanding fish and fishing. Each question and answer may provide a piece to that puzzle on any given fishing day, but to truly become a better fisherman, you must first strengthen your fishing foundation.

Your fishing foundation consists of three areas: approach, attitude, and enjoyment. These three areas are all of equal importance. They must be addressed and strengthened in order to support and organize the large amounts of information available to anglers today. Without a strong foundation, your questions and the answers to them remain as individual pieces to a puzzle.

Approach

Fishing is very easy to over-think. Keep it simple. Approach each problem, no matter how complex it may seem, with the attitude that there are always simple solutions. Keeping fishing simple can be one of the most difficult things to do. With the real facts and information intertwined with advertising and myths, recognizing these true, simple facts can be a major challenge.

Separating facts from advertising, myths, and information designed only to sell products is simple. You must approach each piece of fishing information armed with one fact: fish don't think or make decisions. Fish react to an action. Understanding this, fishing can become quite simple, and the information that can make a real difference becomes quite clear.

> # TROUBLE-SHOOTING TIP
> ## Fish Don't Think
> Whenever you allow yourself to believe that fish think or make decisions, you're about to buy something.

Attitude

The identification of a truly good fisherman is his smile. A smile is your ticket to fishing success. Twenty years ago, you couldn't pass another boat without a wave or a smile, and a friendly, "Hello." You couldn't walk past another fisherman along the bank without getting a smile and a, "How they biting?"

Today, you could call a smiling fisherman an endangered species. Most fishermen don't smile or say, "Hello." They act as though they are the only one on the lake, even though they are in a pack of boats. This is a sad commentary because there's only one thing that can make you a better fisherman, and that's communication. Communication is the sharing of experience and information and is the key to fishing success.

You, as a fisherman, don't have enough fishing days in your lifetime to do all the things that could be and should be done on your favorite lakes, let alone tackling new waters. If you smile, it will open communications and allow knowledge to flow. Join a fishing club, attend a fishing seminar or fish a tournament. These are the things that will make you a better fisherman. Remember: It all begins with a smile.

Enjoyment

Enjoyment is another part of your fishing foundation that must be considered and worked at. Enjoyment and fun don't automatically come with fishing. On the contrary, a fishing trip can at times be a great deal of work and little or no fun. Just ask your wife.

Fishing today has changed dramatically from what it was 20 years ago. Fishing today is too often squeezed into busy schedules, taking something we should enjoy and savor and compressing it into something closer to work than fun. Fishing trips today are high-tech, with all the expensive equipment and the bells and whistles that go with it. Too often time is condensed and restricted. This leaves us without any fun or relaxation, but instead with frustration and a family who hopes they never hear the word "fishing" again!

Today's fishing trips leave much to be desired, as they are generally scheduled to fit into a particular time slot. "We've got to get there by 6:00 A.M. because I have to be back by 3:00 P.M." This means a quick stop for bait (maybe some snacks and ice if you're not in too big a hurry), launch the boat, hit your first hot spot, then the next, and so on. When a fish is eventually caught, it's admired briefly and then quickly tossed back into the water because you don't have enough time to clean it anyway. Soon, the time is up and it's back to the ramp you go. You load the boat and head for home arriving in time for supper. Then at supper, rather than a recap of all the fun you had, you say to your son, "Don't forget to clean the boat." And we wonder why kids don't like to fish anymore!

Twenty years ago fishing was an event that involved the entire family. Planning started about mid-week with deciding where to go. Bait shops were called along with fishing buddies to find where the hot bite "was happening." Kids made sure the grass was mowed and the trash was taken out, being sure not to leave any obstacles that could derail their fishing plans.

Bait gathering was an event, not just something bought along the way to the lake. Snacks weren't bought or picked up at the drive-through along the way. Mom packed the lunch the night before. Fishing was always for the day or until you were done, no time limits. Most of the fish that were caught were kept, and even though they may not have been the biggest, Dad sure acted like it. Dark was the only time we knew to be home, but it was always later than that. First, a stop had to be made at Grandpa's, then Uncle Bill's, showing off the catch-of-the-day. Once home the duties weren't cleaning the boat, but to clean the fish and listen to Mom tell us how she was going to fix the catch for supper. These weren't just fishing trips, but *fishing events* involving the entire family.

How does involving your whole family make you a better fisherman? Simple: you can go fishing more frequently. The more you fish, the more you catch, and the more you catch the better you become, and the more fun you have.

These are the three simple things I consider your fishing foundation: approach, attitude, and enjoyment. Strengthen this foundation and the pieces to the puzzle will fit together.

WHAT'S THE QUICKEST WAY TO INCREASE MY CATCH?

Quite simply, learn how walleyes eat! As a walleye fisherman for well over 30 years and a tournament fisherman for the last 13, I realized only a few years ago that no matter how good a fisherman I was, I can't *make* a walleye bite. It didn't make any difference what tactics or presentations I tried, if a walleye didn't want to bite, he wouldn't. Once I came to this conclusion, I then began concentrating on catching walleyes that *do* want to bite.

Now I had to re-think how I fish and forget about buying products to *make* walleyes bite. Instead, I had to spend time thinking about "What can I do to allow a

QUESTION 2   WHAT'S THE QUICKEST WAY TO INCREASE MY CATCH?

walleye to eat my bait?" To do this I had to understand how walleyes eat.

Let's face it, walleyes don't "short-hit" because they want to. Short-hits are not caused because they look at a bait and say to themselves, "Oh! There's a nightcrawler with a hook in it, I think I'll eat the other end." Give me a break! Fish don't think! Walleyes don't know what a hook is. A walleye merely attempts to eat the whole bait and nothing but the bait if your presentation allows him to do so. If not - that's when the short-hit happens.

If you learn only one thing in this book, learn HOW WALLEYES EAT! Nothing in walleye fishing is as important as this concept. It forms the foundation of our entire "school" of thought, and it affects everything we do when on the water.

How do walleyes eat? I can tell you as I have earlier - walleyes don't "bite" or "nibble." I live in Pierre, South Dakota, just below the tail-races of Oahe Dam. I've spent hundreds of hours fishing below the tail-races in crystal-clear water in the winter time. Just about everything I've learned about walleye fishing is by observing how walleyes eat.

Walleyes typically eat like most "ambush" fish working from a strategic place, in a specific manner. They like structure - rocks, weeds, logs - which help them to eat by allowing them to hide from their prey. Then when unsuspecting baitfish swim a little too close, a walleye will slowly improve his position along the structure and inhale the bait. Does it sound very simple to you? It is!

I *can* tell you what a walleye will *not* do. A walleye will not lash out and bust up a whole school of baitfish like a salmon; he will not dash out and chase his prey with short, powerful lashes like a musky or a northern pike. A walleye will simply ease close to a baitfish, flare its gills open to draw the surrounding water into his mouth and through his gills, and usually bring the bait with that action. Because the baitfish is neutrally-buoyant (it neither sinks or floats), it simply goes with the flow - right into the walleye's mouth. The walleye has another meal with no more energy expended than necessary.

What does this have to do with catching walleyes? Everything. You have to realize that when you attach a fishing line to the bait or lure, you limit the walleye's main weapon for capturing its prey; the line interferes with the natural flow of water, preventing the fish from sucking in your offering. It becomes your fault when a fish short-hits. Once you fully comprehend this vital truth, you'll begin to change your way of angling walleyes, and then you'll catch more fish.

Jig fishing is probably the best example of showing how walleyes eat. A jig fishermen knows that 90 percent of his hits come as the jig is falling. This leads to a popular belief that a fish eases up to the jig and waits for it to fall before he hits it. WRONG! A walleye doesn't care if the jig is falling or rising; he'll hit it just as many times on the way up as when the jig is falling. Again, a walleye makes reactions, not decisions.

What happens is simple, the fishermen lifts the jig, it comes off the bottom and swims through the water. At the same time, a walleye will try to suck in the jig and the surrounding water into its mouth. But, your jigging stroke may merely pull the bait and jig out of the flow of water that is going into the walleye's mouth. Most times a fisherman doesn't even know that this has happened. But, if a fisherman is letting his jig fall when the walleye suck the bait, the jig can easily follow the flow into the walleye's mouth with very little resistance.

Now that you understand how a walleye eats you can concentrate on what you can do to allow your walleye catching success to sky-rocket. Use your imagination and create presentations that allow a walleye to eat easily. With the right attitude and the right presentation, you'll increase your catch tremendously.

WHAT'S THE BEST WAY TO FISH MY HOME LAKE?

How do I fish my favorite lake in my own backyard? What is the best way? THERE ISN'T A BEST WAY! Your favorite lake is for fun and family. Why should you even worry about catching a fish? Whether it's a stock dam just a few hundred yards from the farm house, huge Lake Erie or Michigan, Oahe Reservoir, Mille Lacs, or a host of others, it should be a place to go have fun with family and friends. Forget about catching fish. If that happens, it's a bonus. Your main purpose in being on the water isn't to win a tournament or fill the freezer.

You might "launch" the day with the idea of catching enough for a shore lunch, but if you don't, take the sirloins out of the cooler and start the grill. Boil water for a dozen ears of sweet corn. Sip on your favorite beverage; tell stories; take a nap; listen to the waves lapping against the side of your boat.

Home lakes may include the area closest to the nearest boat landing. Just because a body of water may be extensive in size, you can still enjoy a piece of home territory. Practically living on Lake Oahe and having Lake Sharpe flow about 20 yards from my back door has given me a unique opportunity to study home water. Most of my Lake Sharpe fishing was done from a lawn chair in the backyard with a rod or two out along the beach. With me were my son, daughters, wife and friends; and if we happened to get a bite, all the better.

There are some tips on fishing your home waters that should be remembered. I note these only because they apply to lakes that we know "too well." The old adage "familiarity breeds contempt" is true. You *can* know your own lake "too well." Because you've spent so much time in a lifetime on the lake, your angler, computer mind is probably overloaded with data. If you try to decide what to use, where to go with regard to wind, water temperature, sky, season, color... and the list goes on, you'll just overload. Don't even think about it is my advice. Just load up the boat, grab your kids or friends and go fishing.

On your home lake, size or species is secondary to having fun.

DOES COLOR MAKE A DIFFERENCE?

I n our quest to find a magic bait - one that makes fish bite - colors have been the primary focus and direction. We're in constant pursuit of the right color to make a fish bite. This quest for color has opened a huge market for new products. We have color selectors, thousands of different colored baits, dyes to put on live bait - color, color and more color. Do fish see color as we see it? Who knows? Or for that matter, should we really care?

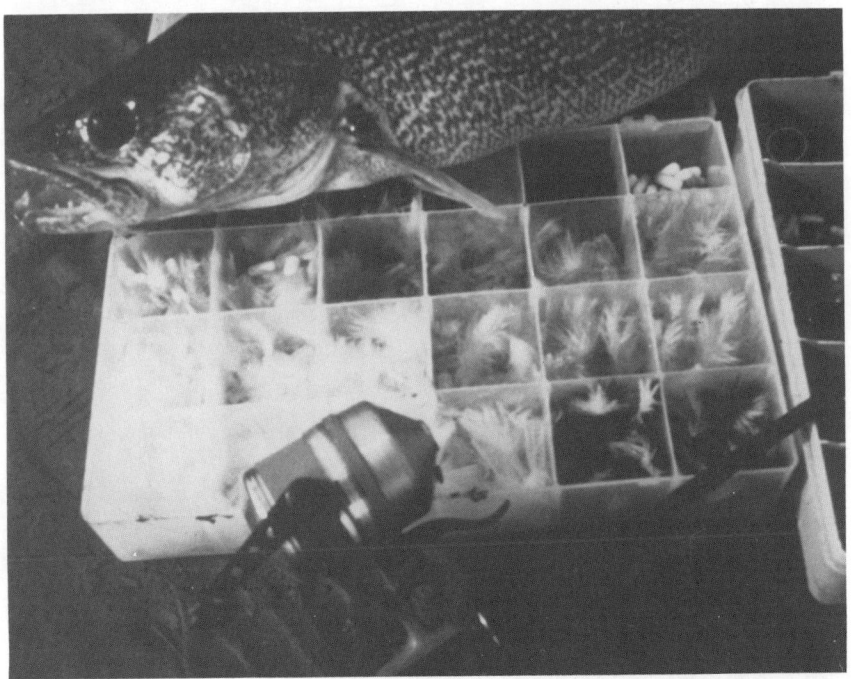

You can argue the merits of color all day. But, if you stick to this one simple rule you can't miss, dark days, dark colors, bright days, bright colors.

Long-time touring pro, Daryl Christensen has mastered the art of jigging, not color.

QUESTION 4   DOES COLOR MAKE A DIFFERENCE?

My personal color selector is very simple. I try different colors and if one works, I stick to it. But, I don't have a set pattern for this. For example, if you and I are out fishing with crankbaits, I may use a chartreuse

> ## TROUBLE-SHOOTING TIP
> ### Walleyes Cannot Relate To Color
> My most troubling thought about color isn't whether or not a fish can distinguish color, but how can he relate to it? How many orange minnows has he eaten? How many chartreuse bugs?

Wally Diver, and you choose an orange one. If you catch a fish on orange, I wouldn't immediately change to orange; however, if you caught two fish, *then I'd change*! You don't have to beat me over the head with color to tell me that it does have some effect on some days. Is it the primary reason for fish to bite? It is highly unlikely.

The color phenomenon is amazing. I don't think we give color a fair chance. For instance, two anglers may start fishing with different colors. When one of them catches a fish, the other immediately changes to that color. We assume that's the color for the day, the color fish want. The real question is - did color make the fish bite or is it that the angler just found active fish? The test for color (which is seldom done) is to change when the fish are hot and biting.

The next time you're digging through your tackle box, searching for the magic color, consider the following thoughts:

1) If fish can see color, what color would they prefer? Studies show that walleyes see chartreuse better than any other color. But how can a walleye relate to this as color? How many chartreuse, blue and white, or fluorescent orange minnows has he eaten? In other words, how do walleyes relate color to food?

2) The next thing to consider is that color couldn't be

a factor at night. The simple reason is that without artificial light at night, you cannot see color. If that sounds a little odd to you, just go to a parking lot with no street lights and only the moon shining overhead. Try to name the colors of the cars. You'll find your results very interesting.

3) Think about how many times you have fished walleyes in water that's not only deep but also murky, stopping light penetration. This basically makes the fish color blind, and again without light, there is no color; as a matter of fact, without light there is no sight.

4) How about dirty water, which is simply small, solid particles suspended in the water? This water doesn't allow any light penetration or vision. Walleyes have fantastic eyes, but they don't have X-ray vision. If we can see only two inches into muddy water, walleyes can only see two inches into muddy water as well. Seeing color, unless the fish are right on top of a bait, cannot be a factor. Another thing to remember is that the nearer the fish are to the bait, the poorer the perception. We can discard the importance of color in a dirty water situation as well.

Yes, color can make a difference, but it will never be a major factor in your angling success. It merely helps you fine-tune your presentations. First you must solve the real problems of location and presentation. After all, you can pull to a spot and change colors as many times as you like, but if there are no fish, you can't catch them, no matter what color you try.

DOES FISH SCENT MAKE WALLEYES BITE?

N^{o!}

16 WALLEYE TROUBLE-SHOOTING

D'Arcy Egan Photo

Joe Hughes, public relations director for PRADCO which is the parent company of Riverside Lures and manufacturer of Gotta Bite, admires a fish that hadda-bite!

DOES FISH SCENT WORK?

Yes! Although nothing *makes* walleyes or any fish bite, something *attracts* them. When you start thinking there's something that makes fish bite, take your wallet out, you're going to buy something, again! Even though fish scent has come a long way in the past couple of years, it's still not the magic bait that *makes* fish bite, but it will definitely have an effect on fishing success.

How? Scent can tip the scales of an indecisive fish in your favor. The biggest advantage with today's scents is after the fact. Once a fish sucks the scented bait into his mouth, taste takes over. Today's scents have incorporated taste stimulants that have a direct effect. They'll cause a fish to hold a bait longer or hit it a second time. Today's scents can take a fish's "Ho-hum attitude" and change it to one of "Got to have it!"

Joe Hughes, public relations director for PRADCO which is the parent company of Riverside Lures and manufacturer of Gotta Bite, sums up the effects of scent the best:

Fish have a sense of smell, and in most species the older and larger the fish, the more refined is their sense of smell. This simple fact has helped create a diverse and populated group of products whose claims sometimes rival those of the old 'Snake Oil' salesman of the nineteenth century.

For the most part, early 'scents' were mostly anise oil or some other type of masking product that covered the human scent. As the business of scent became more competitive, 'scents' became much more sophisticated and effective, they evolved to include 'taste' stimulants which actually suggest to the fish that they are biting on real food such as crawfish, alewife or shad. Today, these 'scent' and 'taste' stimulants are combined together in bottles as well as being impregnated into popular soft-plastic lures.

The leader in this field is Riverside Lures which is the brand name for Real Craw, Real Baitfish, Real Worm and the Gotta Bite taste formula, a registered trademark of Louisiana State University. The process by which these products are produced illustrates the level of scientific involvement that is responsible for the effective quality of today's 'scents' and 'taste' additives.

Real Craw, the first of Riverside scents, was born in the crawfish-rich areas of southern Louisiana. Acadia Products, a Louisiana company, developed and received a patent on a process to derive fluids and oils from crustaceans. This process yields a bottle of real crawfish oil. At Riverside, they say that everything that's a crawfish is in that bottle, except for what a cajun would eat. If you want your jigs and soft plastics to smell like crawfish, there's no better choice than Real Craw. The same type of process also yields Real Baitfish and Real Worm, scents created from the real thing.

Gotta Bite on the other hand, is a 'taste' stimulant that becomes effective when a lure is captured in the mouth of a fish. The development of this product goes far beyond a couple of chemists concocting some secret formula in a back room. Gotta Bite was created after the effective 'mapping' of a bass's brain to determine the actual feeding center of the brain. This open-brain research, conducted at L.S.U., yielded a specific formula that stimulated, to the greatest degree possible, the exact location of a bass' brain that controls feeding. In other words, when a lure with Gotta Bite is captured in a fish's mouth, it is recognized as real food.

The combination of Riverside, Real scents and Gotta Bite creates a scent-taste additive that will increase your fishing success. To use them is to learn first-hand the effectiveness of this new wave of 'taste' and 'scent' products.

DOES TOURNAMENT FISHING AFFECT THE RESOURCE?

That's a great question, and one that I've struggled with the pros and cons of for years. Although I've fished well over 100 tournaments, I've really only looked at fishing tournaments from the position of a participant. Rather than giving you a one-sided answer, I passed this question to Jim Kalkofen.

Jim is presently the executive director of the P.W.T. (Professional Walleye Trail). Prior to this position, he was a public relations officer for Mercury Marine where one of his duties was to direct the Mercury National Walleye Tournament on Lake Winnebago. Along with this duty came the job of answering this precise question to an array of organizations which included state fisheries departments, fishing clubs, conservation groups, the press, and media.

This is Jim's answer:

It's the FACTS that get in the way of any argument about walleye tournament anglers catching too many fish. From years directing the MWC (Manufacturer's Walleye Council), running the Mercury Marine National Walleye Tournament, and heading the In-Fisherman Professional Walleye Trail since 1991, it always comes down to this:

Some anglers catch some fish. It's no different than the average walleye fishing crowd. The only 'on the surface' difference is that tournament anglers bring their catches to one spot at one time. To the casual observer, who sees more fish than he ever caught in his life, it may seem that every fish has been taken from the lake.

Tournament catch rates are not as high as most contestants would like. Limits are seldom landed. In all the PWT tournaments, only one day of one tournament (Lake Erie) did all contestants catch a limit. Usually the catch rates are like Lake Winnebago in 1995, when the PWT operated out of the Pioneer Inn in Oshkosh, WI. The total catch was 1,803 walleyes for 260 contestants. Each person came to the scales with 2.31 walleyes per day. Then, with the assistance of the Wisconsin DNR and PWT technical expert Dick Hackbarth, the contestants released most of these; 1.66 were released each day of the 2.31 that came in.

DNR estimates were that the combined catch and keep number for Lake Winnebago in June was 90,000 walleyes. The PWT anglers, fishing two to a boat (pro and amateur) were responsible for catching and keeping only

QUESTION 7 — DOES TOURNAMENT FISHING AFFECT THE RESOURCE?

506 walleyes. The DNR told the tournament committee which fish could be released. All others were immediately iced, taken to a commercial fish cleaner, filleted and frozen. They were then donated to local charities and needy homes.

Fishing tournaments like the PWT emphasize ELECTIVE harvest. That is, catch fish, but release the bigger walleyes and keep some of the smaller fish for eating. When the fish are biting, it is not necessary to make repeat trips or fill the freezer. Take a fish or two when you want fresh fish, then practice catch and release.

Tournament anglers pay for licenses like every other fisherman; however, tournament daily limits are established less than state limits, which effectively sets total catch limits under what other licensed anglers could put in their boats. Tournament hours are restrictive - no night-time fishing, no evening bite, and only limited time allowed on the water. When the pros arrive in town, they only have a few days to figure out an entire lake system and learn where the walleyes are hiding. The PWT also limits anglers to the number of rods they may use, where they may fishing, how close they may approach other boats. Tournament ethics police their decisions as well.

Tournaments are a proving ground for feat and techniques. They also teach people how to fish. With that knowledge comes a responsibility to practice catch and release. Teach others, especially the younger people you take fishing, that this is the accepted way professionals treat the resource.

Kalkofen's answer has some excellent points, all positive to fishing tournaments. However, I do have concern not necessarily with the tournament itself, but rather the effect it has on local anglers *after* the event. When you bring 200 of the Nation's top walleye anglers together on a single body of water for five or more days, I'll guarantee that they will find the most effective way to catch walleyes. This seems fine as a large percentage of fish are returned during the event and the practice days. It's not what's taken by the professional that concerns me, it's what we've left. What we leave, as tournament professionals, is the knowledge we have accumulated on how to catch huge quantities of large walleyes. This knowledge can hurt the resource. Let me tell you how.

Although the tournament has long been over, the new knowledge of tactics and location continues to catch fish. The only thing that's changed is that it's being used by non-tournament anglers, such as cottage owners, local anglers, guides, and tourists. Think about this the next time the question comes up, does tournament fishing affect the resource - *or do I?*

South Dakota Tourism Photo

Mike McClelland and Al Linder watch the scoreboard.

Part II

WHAT YOU NEED TO BUY

Angling Communications Photo

Top tournament pro, Keith Kavajecz admires the results from a long run on big water.

DO I NEED A $25,000 BOAT?

I don't know if anyone really "needs" a $25,000 boat; however, depending on the area and type of water, many fishermen could use one. Selecting a boat isn't any different than buying a reel or even a hook. Always buy the best tool to do the job.

For example, if the only lake you're going to fish is just a few acres in size and minutes away from home, I would say, "No, you don't need a $25,000 boat." However, as your walleye interests expand, both in distance from home and size of the water fished, the cost of your boat will also expand.

I asked this question to a good friend and top tournament fishing pro Keith Kavajecz. Keith has covered the gamut in fishing boats. From his first 14-foot flat-bottom to the boats that are now required to take advantage of not only the popular, large lakes, but also the equipment available and necessary to fish those lakes, he has used them all. He's also been in the forefront on new product developments by advising manufacturers in boat design and other products to meet the walleye anglers growing needs.

This is Keith Kavajecz response to: "Do I Need A $25,000 Boat?"

Obviously not everyone needs a $25,000 boat - at least not right away! I remember buying my first boat, a 14-foot aluminum with an old, 18 hp outboard and a transom mount electric trolling motor. Between the back two bench seats, I added some wooden shelves so I'd have a place to set my Lowrance Green Box. I also had a portable transducer that swung down on a bracket. The whole package, with trailer, cost me $800 (of course, I got the family discount from my wife's Uncle Reuben). I also re-

member telling my wife this would be the last boat I'd ever need.

Well, 15 years later, with at least an equivalent number of boats, I realized there were a few extra 'features' I was missing in my original purchase. Nowadays I run a state of the art twenty and a half foot boat with a 225 Mercury EFI engine. It has a 9.9 hp, four-stroke 'kicker' (with more power than my original 18 hp), three LCG fish finders, two GPS units with screens that have maps of my location, a 48-pound thrust bow mounted electric motor, a marine band radio, a dual axle trailer, and a price tag between $25,000 and $30,000. Of course I fish for a living!

On the tournament trail, it isn't common for me to run 40, 50 and even 60 miles to get to the winning walleyes. Since tournament days are limited to about nine hours, I need to quickly get to the fish, find my spot, search for walleyes on the electronics and then catch them. That should sound familiar to most fishermen. Very few of us have the luxury to take days or weeks to locate and catch walleyes.

Weekend anglers, in fact, are much like tournament fishermen. They arrive at their destination, search out information at local bait shops, try out the 'hot spots,' locate some areas that are holding fish, and catch some walleyes. All this is done before it's time to head back home. Like anything in this high-tech world, your success or failure at accomplishing these tasks can depend greatly on equipment. Let's take a look at my rig and explain why I, and possibly you, need the gear that I use.

First of all, my boat. I run a big, fast boat because some of the best walleye fishing is in large, expansive bodies of water. The Great Lakes, the Western Reservoirs (Oahe, Fort Peck, Sakakawea), large inland lakes (e.g. Mille Lacs and Winnebago) river systems (e.g. Mississippi, Missouri) and the huge Canadian Shield lakes are the best areas to consistently catch walleyes. Not all regions of these waters hold walleyes; many times the best fishing is out of range for most boats.

QUESTION 8   **DO I NEED A $25,000 BOAT?**   27

A good example of this was at Lake Tobin in Saskatchewan. Rumors of a big fish bite were rampant; so Gary Parsons and I took a late October road trip to the North. The lake basically has one ramp that most anglers use, outside the town of Nippwin. Many anglers were fishing from small boats with low horse power outboards; therefore, most of the fishing pressure was limited to five miles from the landing.

Since our boats could go over 65 miles per hour, running 10 or 15 miles was no big ordeal and took us away from this 'used' water. What did we find? The best big fish bite either of us had ever seen. In one afternoon, we caught a 13 lb, a 14.5 lb, and a 15.7 lb walleye, mixed in with many others over eight. Why did we produce so well? First of all, because we didn't let the boat dictate where we could fish. We were able to go where the fish

Angling Communications Photo

Keith Kavajecz with a nice Saskatchewan walleye.

were! Did we need a fast boat? Of course not, but at a minimum we needed a boat and motor that we were willing to run at least 20 miles. If patient, that may be a 17-foot hull with a 50 hp outboard (about 30 miles per hour). A better choice would be a 17 to 18-foot console boat with a 125 hp engine (40 to 45 miles per hour).

A second reason to run a big boat is for the rough water hazards. Every foot added to the boat's hull will dramatically improve its rough water performance. This is true especially on the Great Lakes where big winds and waves can ruin a day, if not an entire fishing trip. For frequent big water fishing, I suggest a minimum of an 18-foot boat with a 125 hp engine eventually moving up to a 20-foot figerglass boat with a V6 engine. This latter combination will give you the power necessary to outrun bad weather, let you fish on days when small boats will be left on shore, and return you safely back home from rough areas. The boat and motor are the big ticket items when purchasing a rig, but don't skimp on speed and rough water ability.

The next most costly equipment will be your electronics. I live and die by my fish finders! I have three LCG units. I put one on my dashboard (for searching), one on my bow (for when I control the boat with the bow electric), and one in the back of the boat (for trolling). I also run a wider angle transducer of the back unit, so I can see a slightly different view of the bottom and fish than that on my dashboard unit.

To reduce your cost, reduce the number of units but not the functionality of the units purchased. I would buy one high end unit and some spare power cords before purchasing three less functional units. No matter how good your angling skills are, if there are no walleyes where your bait is, you won't catch any walleyes.

The key features to get a good LCG (Liquid Crystal Graph) are: 1) Vertical pixtals; 2) Gray line; 3) Bottom zoom. The best units have 200 vertical pixels and will give you better resolution to see even bottom hugging walleyes. Gray line will help you distinguish the bottom composition and will more easily show fish laying belly to the bottom. A good zoom will show more detail in the zone. Sacrificing any of these features will greatly compromise your ability to find fish.

On the dash and bow units, I have GPS (Global Positioning System) units. These units use satellite information to plot my boat's position, so I can easily keep track of where I am when I locate walleyes. The navigational information also allows me to plot courses back to the landing in case of emergencies (or for weigh-ins).

The most important feature on a GPS unit is a good plotter. It will show an easy to understand picture of all the information and make it a tool for fishing instead of a tool for navigation. On my units (Lowrance's Global Map 2000), the plotter goes one step further in that it shows a map of my location. This allows me to see where my boat is in relation to the shore, islands, etc. that are displayed on the plotter.

A hidden feature to look for on GPS units is a multi-channel receiver. The Lowrance units I have track up to five satellites simultaneously. This gives more accurate and reliable position information. Channels are usually the feature sacrificed in less expensive units. This is not a good place to save money.

How we control walleye boats has undergone a transition over the last decade or so. Pioneered by anglers like Mike McClelland and Gary Parsons, fishing from the bow of a walleye boat, for many reasons, has been the best approach. Because walleye boats are Deep-V (allowing them to run in bigger waves), a strong (24 volt, 48+ lb thrust), long shaft (48+ inches) bow mounted trolling motor is needed. A key element that is often overlooked is the bracket strength of the motors. High thrust and long shafts put unbelievable torque on the brackets. Combine that with the beating the engine takes when running rough water and it's easy to see why a tough engine is required.

The other 'control' engine we use is a 'kicker' engine mounted next to the main outboard. Usually this is a eight to 15 hp and is mainly used for trolling techniques. Often a 'kicker' is one of the first items taken off the 'options' list when there is a budget overrun, maybe rightly so. Unless you're running a 50 hp or less, it's going to be hard to slow a boat down to one mile per hour (my typical trolling speed) with the main engine. If a kicker is not an option, look into using a trolling plate. This device swings a plate down behind the prop and dramatically slows the speed of the boat. When it's time to run, a string is pulled up and the plate swings out of the way.

On my rig I run a 9.9 four-stroke from Mercury. I am often asked if a 9.9 is adequate to control a 20-plus-foot boat. Not only is it more than capable for trolling and boat control, but it also makes a great secondary engine in case of emergencies. The new four-stroke engines are valuable because they do not burn oil in the gas thus eliminating that annoying smoke that filters into the boat. Since the four-strokes are somewhat expensive, don't hesitate to use the eight hp two-strokes. I used them for years without any problems.

Do I need a $25,000 boat? If you fish for a living, fish a great deal, take your walleye fishing very seriously, like to run faster than everyone else on the water, fish big water or are out in big waves often, then the answer is probably YES! Are there excellent compromises in obtaining a rig that will perform well in most situations? Of course.

Just remember to try to pick equipment that will not limit your fishing success. Purchase a boat that can handle some big water and have enough speed to maneuver you comfortably to the walleyes. Spend a little extra money on good electronics, and remember, even if you tell your wife this is the last boat you'll ever need, it probably isn't. (You can always correct your mistakes in boat two, three, or four.)

I couldn't have said it better myself, but that's OK. I don't have to "say" anything better than Keith, just fish better!

WHY IS BOAT CONTROL CRITICAL?

Good boat control is so vital to walleye fishing that the difference between good and poor boat control can be the determining factor in your fishing success. Walleye fishing demands better boat control than any other kind of fishing. Why? Because in walleye fishing, anglers routinely use their boat as part of their presentations. Boat control equals presentation.

Daryl Christensen uses his bow mount electric to control his boat in current.

> ## TROUBLE-SHOOTING TIP
>
> A sea anchor can change a random drift into an exact presentation.
>   Sea anchors are an important part of boat control while drift fishing. It will slow your speed while drifting and trolling providing you have the proper equipment. It is important to purchase a sea anchor that is large enough to do the job. Most manufacturers recommend sizes that are too small to handle today's walleye boats. My personal preference is the Slow Poke sea anchor by Quick Change Systems.
>   As far as positioning the sea anchor for boat control, the placement of the sea anchor while drifting sideways with the wind is important. To drift directly with the wind, the sea anchor must be dead center. To drift to the right, move the sea anchor to the left of center of your boat: for drifting left reverse the procedure.
>   The advantage of using a sea anchor vs. backtrolling is very simple: a sea anchor allows you to drift sideways with the wind. This controlled drift will allow you to spread out your lines and cover more area, thus putting the odds in your favor when fishing scattered fish.

Learning good boat control is easy; it's just a matter of practice. Manipulating your boat is something you already do every day on the water. *Good* boat control is simply a matter of manipulating your boat during certain wind and water conditions to present the bait in an effective manner. Learning good boat control will lead to big payoffs in your fishing success.

Let's briefly look at some boat control options that will help increase your catch:

Drifting

There are several ways to drift for walleyes. Using the wind or current is simply a great way to catch scattered, active fish. But, what if your fish aren't positioned right for a natural drift? You'll need another type of boat control.

Controlling your drift with a Slow Poke sea anchor (Slow Poke is made by Quick Change Systems), is a great solution. The Slow Poke gives great drift control, both by slowing the boat speed and the drift direction. Each Slow Poke has several tow ropes used to swing the boat into proper alignment with the wind in order to achieve the desired drift direction. Don't worry, it's very simple to use and with a little practice will put you in complete control.

Bow Mount Electric

Controlling drifts with a bow-mounted electric trolling motor is my favorite method. The MotorGuide Beast (which uses 36 volts) gives me control in about every situation. It allows the boat to be positioned in the best drifting course over points, weedlines, or flats. With practice, boat control with an electric becomes second nature. The way you know you have complete control is when you have to fish without one. You can't!

Backtrolling

Backtrolling is simply a method of boat control that "pulls" your boat backward through the water as opposed to "pushing" it forward. It makes an effective difference if you're fishing in a heavy wind. When trolling forward, the wind will usually swing the bow of the boat, and you'll be continually "chasing" your bow to push it back into the trolling path. This is definitely not good boat control.

By going backwards, you can put your bait right where you want it to be. This works the same way as a bow mounted electric does. It "pulls" you through the water giving you maximum boat control with a minimal effort.

Add a flasher to the transom for the best way to follow underwater structure. I use Humminbirds Pro-Flasher, and coupled with backtrolling, the Pro-Flasher allows me to use a precise and perfect backtrolling presentation.

Forward Trolling

Forward trolling is another method of presentation in which you use boat control. Fishing crankbaits on a forward troll allows you to move faster and spread your baits over a wider area then do other presentations.

The "S" shaped troll is also an effective trolling pattern, and you'll cover a great deal of water quickly. The "S" trolling pattern is the ideal crankbait presentation. As the turns are maneuvered, the outside lines tighten and speed up the bait possibly triggering an aggressive fish into a "chase." The inside lines slow down and create slack. They then become neutral buoyant, which is the best presentation I know to allow a fish to eat the bait.

Anchoring

Yes, anchoring is boat control and can be effective in walleye fishing. Slip bobbering is a successful stationary anchor presentation enabling you to put your bait right into the fish zone on reefs, weedlines and trees.

Anchoring as boat control can be more that just "parking" your boat on the water. By working with the wind, you can use your anchor along with a long rope to position your boat at intervals along reefs or other structures that are holding fish. A 75 to 150-foot rope will allow you to anchor your boat upwind of your designated structure. Let out 20 to 25 feet of rope, fish the surrounding area, let out more rope, fish the next length of area, and continue the procedure until you cover the entire area or run out of rope. Then pull up and start all over again.

WHAT ELECTRONICS SHOULD I BUY?

Electronics are a standard piece of equipment for today's angler. They are our windows in the water, our underwater eyes.

By opening those windows with electronics, you will be a more effective fisherman. Electronics allow you to determine depth, structure, and most importantly, the location of fish. With such an array of electronics available today, choosing the units right for you can seem like a monumental task. Should you choose to take on the task of reviewing each product on the market, studying operational manuals, comparing features, cost and values, I'm afraid that by the time you've reached a decision not only would the fishing season be nearly over, but the unit selected might well be obsolete!

TROUBLE-SHOOTING TIP

Fish Finders?

No matter what features your electronics offer or how much the cost, electronics can't find fish. They can only tell you when *you have* found fish!

With accelerated technology and new product developments, an array of units appear annually. Although confusing, it doesn't mean the one you purchased last year isn't operable this year. On the contrary, the electronic industry has reached such a level of perfection that new product changes are very small. Your older units are not only still good, but also improve each time you use them.

Forget the bells and whistles; choose electronics to fit

TROUBLE-SHOOTING TIP

Electronics Are Only As Good As You Are

It doesn't make any difference what type of electronics you choose or how much money you spend, your equipment is only as valuable as the amount of time you invest in learning how to use it.

your needs. Those needs are generally created by two factors: the type of water to be fished and the methods of angling to be used.

Consider the type of water first:

Rivers

Rivers require the bare minimum in electronics. Usually shallow, the river current is the key to where fish will hold. Flasher-type units are adequate in this situation. A flasher is ideal for reading depth at any speed and following a break-line as you drift. My choice is Humminbird's Jimmy Houston Pro Flasher.

Lakes

With lakes offering more variety in structure and depth, your electronics' needs will increase. You will still need a flasher for pin-point boat control and for reading actual fish on structure along with the structures' shape. A good LCD or LCG display depth sounder is a must. My personal preference is Humminbird's 3D Wide Vision.

Reservoirs

Reservoirs require basically the same needs as lakes, except you may want to throw in a GPS unit. Although out-of-water structures on reservoirs are great for visually marking hot spots, safety also becomes an issue. Reservoirs can be huge and visual points of reference can look alike. It is very easy for an angler to become confused, even without a storm or fog.

Open Water Basins

Leave your flashers at home! This type of fishing demands an LCD or LCG with the widest cone angle possible. When trying to find scattered schools of walleyes in vast areas of open water, wide angle transducers have a major advantage. Once you've located fish, keeping track of your location and that of the fish is the key. A GPS will not only keep track of your school of fish, but it will get you home safely and back to the fish tomorrow. My choice is the Humminbird NS10 GPS.

TROUBLE-SHOOTING TIP

Every Fish Is A Walleye!
When marking fish on your electronics, don't try to determine species by size, quantity or relationship to the structure. Consider every fish a walleye and fish it with a confidence and determination to make it bite!

38 WALLEYE TROUBLE-SHOOTING

Although you're fishing presentation should be the number one reason for the type of electronics you choose, the type of fishing you'll be doing also weighs on your decision. Consider the following presentations:

Jigging: Use flashers for pin-pointing accuracy in boat positioning.

Rigging: Use LCD's or LCR's for your needs to see the whole picture.

Bottom Bouncers: Use flashers for simply following the correct depth.

Trolling: I like all three: LCD, LCR, plus GPS. Not only do I have to take a look at a great deal of water, but also I want to go safely home so I can return to the fish another day.

TROUBLE-SHOOTING TIP

Accelerate Your Learning

The quickest way to learn your electronics is to leave your rods at home. Go to a clear water lake where you can see the bottom to at least 10 feet. Simply compare what you can see visually with how your electronics reports it. If you see rocks, watch how your electronics record rocks. The same applies to detecting weeds, brush, and even the bottom. This can accelerate your learning process by five years.

DO I NEED A GPS?

The need for a GPS presents a tough, popular question. A good friend of mine, Steve Nelson from Pierre, South Dakota, who writes for numerous outdoor publications, was also considering this question for a magazine article. Here was his answer to the question: "Do I need a GPS?"

Of course you do, especially if you fish tournaments or big bodies of water like Lake Erie or Michigan.

GPS stands for Global Positioning System. It's a constellation of satellites that twice a day transmit precise time and position. If you have an instrument that can receive this information, you can be anywhere on earth

Humminbird's NS-10 GPS.

> ## TROUBLE-SHOOTING TIP
> ### A GPS Isn't Radar
> When navigating in fog, be careful of floating and submerged obstructions and, most of all, other boats. The GPS will get you home, but it's not radar.

and determine your precise location. It also enables you to mark an area, within a few feet, where you have caught fish and to go back to that exact spot the next day, or the next year. For example, let's say I'm fishing Lake Erie in a big walleye tournament. During pre-tournament fishing, I've found a large reef five miles out in the middle of nowhere, and it's loaded with fish. No problem. I just us my Hummingbird NS-10, (which by the way has mappings of U.S. inland lakes already built right into it), punch in the coordinates, and return to exactly the same spot the next day by the shortest possible route.

GPS is an essential part of nearly every pro-angler's gear, and it will soon become standard equipment on every boat. It's a time saver, a locator, and a navigating device. For example, you head out on Lake Erie; and fog is predicted for the day. Without a GPS, you might think twice about going fishing; however, you know you can return safely to port with a GPS. They are available in hand held units and permanent units like the NS-10.

The GPS was developed by the Department of Defense. Today it is used by anyone who needs to know the precise time or the exact location of people or objects. There are many systems available including Hummingbirds and Magellans. Each year the GPS is becoming more and more popular not only as a locator, but also as a life saver.

Steve gave a great explanation on what a GPS is and why you need it. Now let me tell you why you should buy one. Safety! Whether you are on the Great Lakes, a midwestern reservoir, or even a smaller glacial lake in

> ## TROUBLE-SHOOTING TIP
> ### A GPS Only Knows What You Tell It
> When a storm develops and visibility is bad, your NS-10 will get you home, provided you leave before the water becomes too rough, and you remembered to punch in your home weigh point as you left.
>
> Although global positioning will get you back where you want to be, remember structure can change. In less than a year, Lake Oahe in South Dakota dropped 25 feet and created thousands of miles of new shoreline.
>
> Your weigh point from last season may no longer be a hot spot. As a matter of fact, it could have grass growing on it.

Minnesota, losing your direction is easy. A cloudy day, a gentle, mid-day wind change or fog can suddenly engulf your boat. Even the most experienced angler can become confused. A GPS will straighten you out and point you in the right direction. In conjunction with your marine band radio or cellular phone, a GPS can provide an accurate location for help to come to you in case of engine trouble or a medical emergency.

If the safety factor alone doesn't make you dig into your pocket to buy a GPS, maybe another reason will - communications. How many times have you tried to follow a hot tip only to end up frustrated. For example, your buddy calls and says, "The bite is on, we killed 'em." Then he proceeds to give you the *exact* directions: "First go to the "can't-miss-it" boat ramp, then after you launch, turn right (right when you're standing on the boat dock or when you're sitting in your boat?), go three miles (three miles following the shoreline, a bee-line or four miles?), you'll see a dead tree on shore (of course, there's a dead tree every 50 feet), go straight out 450 yards (a quarter of a mile, four and a half football fields, or a little too far for me to shoot a deer?) and you're there!" Wrong! You never arrived, and you never will unless you have a GPS. By the way, that same hot tip in GPS language goes something like this, "The bite is on, here's the numbers! Oh! By the way, I left a small bobber floating there, would you pick it up for me?" No problem.

South Dakota Tourism Photo

Outdoor writer, Steve Nelson, definitely wants to find this spot again.

HOW DO YOU CHOOSE THE RIGHT ROD?

When selecting a rod, the most important thing to do is to realize you're not just buying a fishing rod, you're selecting an instrument to perform a particular function.

Selecting a rod isn't any different from selecting a tool to remove a part from your automobile. You wouldn't start by going to the tool box and selecting three wrenches just because they were made by Snap-On and very expensive. Chances are you'll find that if the wrench doesn't fit, it's not possible to complete the job correctly. You must first look at your car and identify the nuts and bolts that must be replaced. Then, and only then, can you select the size and shape of the tool to do the best job. (If they happen to be made by Snap-On, that's great!)

Selecting the appropriate fishing rod is no different from selecting the proper tool to repair your car. You must first identify the basic functions you expect your rod to perform for a particular fishing technique. To recognize these basics is not always easy. Choice is usually clouded with sales hype, price, promises to catch more fish to what your buddy thinks and "what kind of rod your dad has used."

My formula for rod selection is simple. Choose rods one at a time for a particular technique. Only then can you identify the characteristics you need for a rod - design, length and action. When these key parts are addressed with common sense, rod selection becomes easy.

Let me list, by fishing techniques, my five picks for walleye rods. I think you'll agree that choosing rods for a *specific* reason makes rod selection not only simple, but correct.

> ## TROUBLE-SHOOTING TIP
> ### The Best Rods Are Self-Destructive
> I think we can all agree that the best rod we've ever seen was the one that "Dad" had. It was like magic, producing the most and the biggest fish, anywhere at anytime. This rod was so special that you couldn't wait to give it a try. At the first opportunity, when Dad was out of sight, it was yours for the day. Then the unthinkable happened. It broke - it just broke - you didn't do anything; it just self-destructed.
>
> Self-destruction is bad enough, but the one my dad had also disintegrated; once it was found tucked away into the corner of the stairs. Unfortunately for me, the "disintegration" took place on my backside.

Jigging: Quantum QXLS56MW

Design - Spinning

There are no options here. Because of light line requirements, an open face spinning reel is a must. Add this to the comfort and balance you get from spinning reels and the choice is easy.

Length - 5'6"

Since jig fishing is 90 percent eye contact with your fishing line, a short rod will not only move your focal point (the tip) closer, but also allows for quick and exact rod tip placement avoiding wind and light glare off the water for easier reading. Control is another key factor to jig fishing. A short rod offers more tip control not only for vertical jigging, but also for casting light line and baits less than a quarter ounce.

Action - Medium

This is the perfect action for a jigging rod. It has enough stiffness to resist the slightest "tick," but yet is soft enough not to break light line on the hook-set. It also has the backbone (the rod bends to a certain point) to control a "frisky" fish with light line.

Rigging: Quantum Tour Edition TS704FW

Design - Spinning

The balance and comfort of an open face reel are the keys to this technique. Add this to the physical demand of releasing line to let a fish run and a spinning rod and reel is the only choice.

Length - 7'0" (one piece)

A rigging rod should be long yet comfortable and controllable. Length is the key factor with this presentation giving you the ability to take up slack line, absorb line stretch, and still deliver hook-setting power.

Action - Medium

This medium action rod has plenty of hook-setting power, but yet a fast tip for easy reading. It allows you to distinguish the bottom from a fish. Add the fast tip to its length, and you have the maximum reaction time needed before the fish feels enough pressure to become alarmed.

Crankin': Quantum Tour Edition TC665FW

Design - Baitcaster

A bait-casting rod in combination with a good bait-casting reel will allow comfort and take the work out of endless hours of casting. Add to this control and the rod's ability to cast heavy line, the TC665FW out performs any other design.

Length - 6'6" (one piece)

This length is long enough to offer maximum casting distance yet short enough for good accuracy and control.

Action - Medium

This medium action will provide a good solid backbone for hook penetrating power. The hook setting ability is more important on a crankbait rod than any other. Most techniques require setting one hook, but on a crankbait you can have six to twelve hooks to set. Another advantage to consider is a fast tip, a major aid in casting distance. Let your rod do some of the work!

Trolling - Quantum QXLC79MW

Design - Baitcaster

This is a medium heavy baitcasting rod that combined with a husky bait-casting reel is stiff enough to handle all trolling paraphernalia from planer boards to drop weights to lead-core line to deep-diving lures. Yet, it still has plenty of action left when a fish hits, allowing for an automatic hook-set even while the rod is still in the rod holder.

Length - 7'9" (one piece)

A long rod is the real key when trolling. The length not only allows you to spread rods out to cover more water, but also lets you elevate the rod's tip as high as possible, which is a major advantage with trolling techniques that deal with planer boards and skis. Another consideration is that you *visually* fish these rods; in other words, the rods will be in rod holders and not in your hands. The longer the rod, the easier it is to read and the more time you have to react.

Action - Medium Heavy

Don't forget how you're going to be using this rod and all the equipment it could be towing. A medium heavy trolling rod offers a uniform bend from tip to handle. This allows the entire rod to respond once a fish hits and offers maximum hooking ability while still in the rod holder.

Bottom Bouncer - Quantum Tour Edition TS864MW

Design - Spinning

In the past, the design of bottom bouncer rods was simple. It was a matter of preference with no demonstrated advantages for either spinning or bait-casting. The design has changed with the refinement of the technique. Now, with the Lite-Bite system of bottom bouncers (Lite Bite is a system of bottom bouncers that slips and allows you to feed line to a finicky walleye) you

QUESTION 12 HOW DO YOU CHOOSE THE RIGHT ROD?

have the ability to open the bail and release free-flowing line. This is a must! It also makes a spinning rod the only choice possible when using bottom bouncers.

Length - 8'6" (two piece)

Most bottom bouncer fishing is done with the rod in a holder, so again it is a technique that has to be visually fished. Long rods give you more time to react and can be easy to read. Couple this with their ability to spread your lines out when trolling or drifting, and you'll agree that longer is better. Remember that a two piece rod is the key - an eight and one-half foot, one-piece rod just wouldn't fit in your rod box.

Action - Medium Light

The lighter the rod the quicker it will react to a light biting fish or a snag. This gives you extra time to respond. It also offers a uniform bend with a long, soft sweep that allows you to take up slack, a major problem with bottom bouncers, and produce a solid hook-set.

Mike chooses the best rod for the job!

48 WALLEYE TROUBLE-SHOOTING

Steve Nelson Photo

DO LONG RODS REALLY HELP?

Other than my boat, motors and electronics, the one thing that helps me catch more fish is my eight or nine-foot walleye rods.

The most obvious place to use a long rod is when trolling. Trolling is simply running a bait past scattered fish. The object of trolling is to present a bait to as many fish as possible. Many times I'll see anglers trolling with two rods over the transom and a rod over each side. These fishermen will only cover an area of about 12-feet wide behind the boat. By using a long rod set out on each side of the transom, you can cut a swath about 25-feet wide and cover twice the area.

If you put your bait past twice as many aggressive fish, it is just logical that your chances of catching more fish will increase dramatically. Trolling is a numbers game, the angler who places his bait in the strike zone in front of more fish is going to catch more. Long rods spread baits allowing twice the coverage and twice the fish.

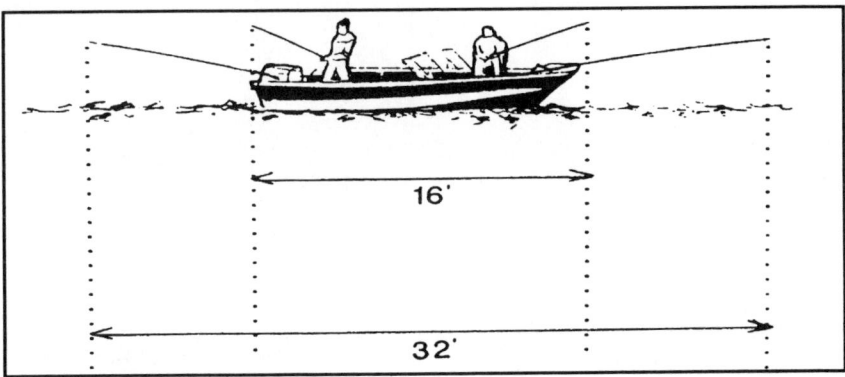

Long rods can increase your coverage by 100 percent if you use them correctly.

50 WALLEYE TROUBLE-SHOOTING

Long rods for kids - works!

South Dakota Tourism Photo

TROUBLE-SHOOTING TIP

Long Rods For Kids

The bonus of long rods will be realized whenever the kids go fishing with you (I hope this occurs frequently in your boat). Kids have a terrible habit of quickly becoming preoccupied with "things." They'll put their rod down, lean them against the boat or sometimes place them in a rod holder.

Subconsciously when fishing with kids, you may end up fishing their rods too. You're watching their rod to see if it's on the bottom, how much line is out, and most importantly, did a fish hit? Longer rods are easier to read and they permit more reaction time from the initial bite to setting the hook. A long rod is also much more forgiving if it snags or a fish makes a run. Long rods can make a kid look like a pro when it comes to handling fish. It also makes Dad's life much easier!

Another opportunity to land more walleyes with long rods is while drifting. The same principle still applies as in trolling. While wind drifting or controlled drifting on structure, don't set four rods over the side of the boat and settle for covering an area of 15 feet wide with your drift. Put a long rod out off the bow and another out the stern. This will allow you to cover over twice the water, or over 30 feet. By using old math or a calculator, it all computes the same; cover twice the area and catch

---

TROUBLE-SHOOTING TIP

Purchasing Long Rods

Downrigger rods make excellent walleye rods. My first long rod was an economical Eagle Claw downrigger rod that served me very well. Since then, improvements with graphite have led me to select the Zebco Rhino downrigger rod which not only fits into the budget, but also are virtually destruction proof. With youngsters in the boat, I'd really look at the Rhino. Zebco recently developed an eight and a half foot rod with the walleye angler in mind - the new Quantum bottom bouncer rod, model QXLS94ML. This is my personal choice for a second rod; however, as you consider a brand name rod, the number one thing to look for is length.

---

twice the fish.

You should also use a long rod as your second rod. In most states, two rods are allowed. Some states may permit three while some allow an unlimited number. Minnesota only allows the use of one.

When you have the opportunity to use two rods, you'll quickly realize that two rods are harder to handle than one. Many fishermen are much better off fishing with one and concentrating on that one rod. My suggestion is to learn to use a primary rod which is the rod in your hand. Give it 95 percent of your attention. Whether rig-

QUESTION 13   DO LONG RODS REALLY HELP?

Bob Propst, Sr., may not have invented long rods, but he definitely discovered many of the uses for them in walleye fishing.

ging, jigging or using a bottom bouncer, your primary rod deserves all your attention. If you choose to use a second rod, use a long rod and rig it safe.

What I call "rigging safe," is very simply rigging your second rod so it doesn't *cause* problems. In other words, rig it so it doesn't snag. A snag-free rig can still keep the bait in the fish zone a foot or two off the bottom and provide you with those bonus fish.

When I'm using a long rod as a second rod, here's how I rig it. I tie on a Lite Bite bottom bouncer, which is a wire weight system that's almost snag free because only the wire touches the bottom. Attached to the bottom bouncer is a four or five-foot leader with a plain hook or a floating jig head. A floating jig head will keep the bait off the bottom and allow you to keep bait in the fish zone without becoming snagged.

Because your second rod is in a rod holder and not in your hand, it must be visually fished. The big advantage of long rods for walleyes is that they are forgiving and easy to read. You'll learn very quickly that if you snag, long rods will gently bend at a constant speed. This generally allows plenty of time to swing the rod back behind the snag and free it. In shallow water you can actually reach the length of the rod into the water and most times work your bait out of the rocks or off a branch.

With an eight or nine-foot rod, you can also read when a fish is on. The rod is very soft and gentle, and the fish won't find stiff resistance as the rod slowly bends. When this happens, the angler has time to reach the rod and set the hook. You'll be amazed as how many fish you can catch with the long rod in a holder!

Long rods will put the walleye odds in your favor. Even though an eight or nine-foot rod may not fit the image of what most fishermen want to purchase, it is by all means a "good" walleye rod. If you happen to have a chance to check out a professional walleye tournament anglers' boat, I'd be willing to bet every one has at least one long rod.

WHAT KIND OF LINE SHOULD I USE?

This question was probably one of the first questions I was ever asked at a fishing seminar. It still remains one of the most frequently asked.

In the last 20 years, monofilament fishing line has improved by leaps and bounds. Although huge advertising budgets keep fishing line in the forefront of anglers' thoughts with words such as "new," "improved," "sensitive" and "super," monofilament fishing line is close to reaching the point of "near-perfection."

If you took the leading manufacturers' products including the newest, the most sensitive, the strongest, the limpest and the most improved, put them all in a box, shook them up, dumped them in a pile and picked just one, you would have an excellent quality fishing line.

Choose whatever brand you like, the one in which you have the most confidence. I use Silver Thread. I won't tell you that it's the best, but I'll guarantee that I won't switch. I learned many years ago (through the school of hard knocks and broken lines) that your line doesn't break because of bad line, but because of bad maintenance. Take care of your fishing line and pay attention to the details. Keep your fishing line away from as much direct sunlight and excess heat as possible. Make it a habit to test your knots. Periodically run your

---

TROUBLE-SHOOTING TIP

Broken Line?
The next time a lunker departs with your favorite lure, think about this: Fish don't break fishing line, people do!

thumbnail down the last few feet and check for nicks. By all means check the line after each boat ride or trip in the truck. It's easy to check your line for strength: try to break it. If you think it may have broken too easily, compare it to a spool of new line. If there's a difference, it's time to change your line and check your reel drag!

Maintenance and paying attention to detail is the secret to good fishing line. When selecting fishing line, line size (pound test) is more important than brand name. Select the line size that will offer you the qualities that best supports the type of fishing you'll be doing.

Let's look at four key walleye presentations and the size of fishing line that best supports them:

Jigging: 6# Test

Small line diameter plays a key part in jig fishing. The smaller the line diameter, the easier it is for a fish to suck in the jig and eliminate short-hits. Six-pound test seems to be the perfect marriage between strength and diameter.

Some anglers choose four-pound test, but I feel the increase in line stretch with this smaller diameter hampers your ability to set the hook.

A few anglers use two-pound test. They're just kidding themselves and others; they really don't want to catch any walleyes!

Trolling: 14# Test

Larger diameters of line have less stretch and are much better for hook-sets, particularly when the rod is in a rod holder. The other advantages of a stronger trolling line is that you'll be able to pull a few more lures from snags that you would normally lose with a lighter line. At about "five dollars a pop," that's important.

Bottom Bouncer: 12# Test

Line diameter has very little effect on bottom bouncer presentations. Heavier line diameter does offer extra strength to pull away from snags and give minimal line stretch which is critical when hook-setting.

Lindy Rigs: 6# Test

The Lindy rig presentation demands the same school of thought as jigging. Lighter line has less resistance in the water and allows a semi-active fish the opportunity to suck in the bait and swim away with the least amount of resistance.

Selecting the right line size is easy, just consider the job that you want it to perform.

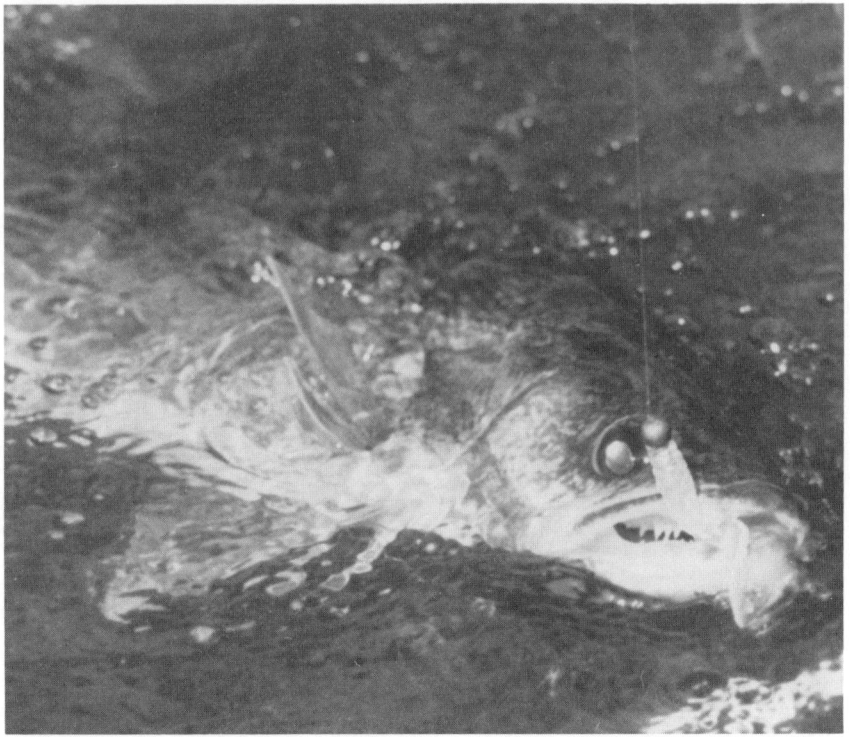

Steve Nelson Photo

Light Line is the key for finicky walleyes.

58 WALLEYE TROUBLE-SHOOTING

Mark Romanack Photo

SHOULD I CHANGE TO THE NEW SUPER LINES?

When the super lines first appeared on the store shelves a couple of years ago, I wasn't particularly impressed by their performance or by their outrageous price tag. However, huge improvements have been made in just a short time. Improvements not only in quality, but in price, have assured a place for super lines, and they are here to stay.

Super lines offer smaller line diameter with greater strength and a minimum stretch that complements several walleye presentations. Even though these qualities are attractive, beware; they are not magic. They won't replace the top quality monofilaments needed for *every* type of walleye presentation. The super lines have a no-stretch quality (whether this quality is a positive or negative is beside the point), that has to be addressed. We have spent the last 50 or more years fine-tuning our fishing systems, from the tip of the hook to how the handle of the rod fits our hand. These characteristics have all been developed around "line stretch."

Hooks are designed to penetrate with a soft, constant pressure allowed by line stretch and rod action. This incorporates line stretch as part of a shock absorber system, especially when handling a struggling fish. The rod's action was also built to consider and complement line stretch.

Reels were designed to use the memory characteristics found in monofilament to aid in casting. State-of-the-art bait-casters were designed to take advantage of the larger diameter and weight of monofilament lines. Even our attitudes and physical actions involved in casting and hook-setting have been formed around line that stretches. Changing from monofilament to the new super lines means changing more then just your line.

You'll find when changing to the new super lines for jigging, a presentation that benefits tremendously, you'll have to change rods. The line stretch that's lost has to be replaced, and in jig fishing this is done by using a longer, medium action, softer rod.

The technique that receives the most benefits from the super lines is trolling. Again, if you change the line, change the rod. Because of the minimum stretch qualities of the new super lines, lure action is transmitted exceptionally well to your rod tip when trolling. This enhances the tip action, telling you not only if you have a fish on or a hit, but also that your lure is clear of any weeds.

Remember, no-stretch means exactly that - no-stretch! Use your drag as a shock absorber! Use super light drags that allow the line to slip as the fish struggles or when you're snagged. With no-stretch line, something has to give; I hope it's not your rod!

South Dakota Tourism Photo

Tony Dean and Mike McClelland discuss the pros and cons of the new super lines.

WHY DO YOU USE LIGHT LINE?

When fishermen talk about the type of line they use with jigs or live bait rigs for walleyes, they say: "Always use light line for walleyes." When they bring up the light line issue, I ask them: "Why do you use light line for walleyes?" Most fishermen don't know the answer. Others will say that walleyes can't see the lighter line or feel it.

Using light line, especially when jigging, *is* the right presentation to use, but most fishermen are doing it for all the wrong reasons. Stop and really think about it! Is heavier line really easier to see than light line? I can

Mike McClelland with an early spring walleye that fell victim to light line.

see the lighter line just as well as the heavy line in water, and I think a walleye can as well. As a simple and logical fisherman, I can't believe a walleye is smart enough to judge the weight of different fishing lines. The walleye doesn't even know what it is! I also can't imagine a walleye saying: "There's a fishing line which has a deadly bait that will catch me."

Another statement I often hear from fishermen about light line is that walleyes have a harder time feeling light line. These fishermen say that "walleyes feel the heavier line and spit out the bait." I have difficultly assigning any merit to this thought. Why would a walleye worry about a tiny piece of fishing line when there are similar things in his environment like weeds, moss, and reeds? What if the walleye feels the fishing lines in his mouth. Who cares? By the time a walleye would realize that this is a fishing line, he probably already has a Wally Diver, a jig or a hook in his mouth.

If light line didn't make a difference, I would use 25-pound test all of the time. Not only would this allow me to pull the fish right over the side of the boat, but I could also save hundreds of dollars a year in tackle. I'd probably never lose another expensive crankbait or even a cheap jig, and fishing nets would be history.

The most important reason we use light monofilament line for walleyes is because of its small diameter which allows a bait to flow easily into the walleye's mouth. To understand this better, we must again look

TROUBLE-SHOOTING TIP

Walleyes Aren't Smart

Never give walleyes credit for being smart or being able to relate a fishing presentation to a dangerous situation. If walleyes had this intellectual ability, we wouldn't have to worry about the illegal netting occurring. Wouldn't you think that if walleyes could see and identify fishing line, they would surely be able to recognize a deadly gill net?

at how walleyes eat.

Knowing that a walleye inhales a bait rather than biting it, we can present a bait to the walleye that will allow them to eat it. Light line is the answer because it allows the bait to flow easily into the fish's mouth when he inhales the water surrounding it. This is where light line or a smaller line diameter plays its part in walleye fishing. Walleyes like to ease up to within a few inches

Jim Kalkofen Photo

Tournament pros, Jerry Anderson and Bruce Sampson show the results of light line and slip bobbers on early season fish.

of the bait. By flaring their gills and opening their mouths at the same time, they suck in the surrounding water, and the bait flows with it into the open mouth.

If the bait weren't attached to a fishing line, it would easily move into the walleyes mouth. But, we do have line attached. The heavier the fishing line, the more resistance it creates and the more difficult it becomes for walleyes to suck in the bait. This simply adds up to a "short-hit." A "short-hit" merely means that the fish is sucking in the water that surrounds the bait and not getting any of the bait.

If lighter fishing line with a smaller line diameter is used, resistance becomes less, and the bait will now flow easily into the walleye's mouth with ease and eliminate many short-hits. When the line's resistance has prevented the bait from moving to the fish's mouth with the flow of water, all the walleye gets is the tail end of your bait - the *end* without a *hook*! Remember, fish never try to eat just half the bait. The fish has tried as hard as he could to get the *whole* bait into his mouth. The bait started to move with the flow into the walleye's mouth, but that heavy line resistance only allowed the free end of the bait to move.

Whenever you have a "short-hit," it's your fault. A short-hit is a very strong message to lighten up, use smaller diameter line, lighter jigs, and lighter baits. My line choice for early spring walleyes on small jigs is four-pound test Silver Thread.

Another problem you'll experience with light line is difficulty with setting the hook. The remedy is long rods. With long rods, you can put more pressure on the fish and eliminate shock on the line. Their are dozens of long rods from which to choose; I personally like Quantum's Tour Edition 7' medium action (TS704F).

Remember, all you have to do is keep an open mind, apply common sense, and search for simple answers. Smaller line diameter is one of those simple answers to catching "short-hitting" walleyes.

WHAT KNOTS ARE FOR WHAT?

Unless you're working on a Boy Scout merit badge, knot tying is probably not high on the list of exciting things to master. On the other hand, losing a big fish to a slipped knot does give an added incentive to learn how to tie a knot correctly.

Knots are a fact of fishing, especially in walleye angling, and are a small but vital part of every presentation. Learning to tie the correct knots for a given presentation is fundamental to being a successful angler. Learn the knot to do the job.

Surgeon's Knot

A surgeon's knot is a simple two-overhand knot. It's the quickest way to connect new line to the backing of the reel.

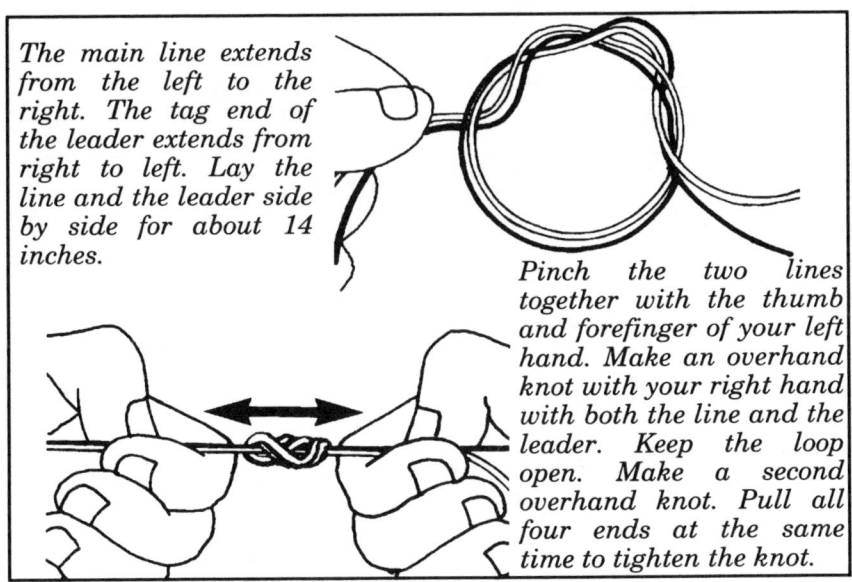

The main line extends from the left to the right. The tag end of the leader extends from right to left. Lay the line and the leader side by side for about 14 inches.

Pinch the two lines together with the thumb and forefinger of your left hand. Make an overhand knot with your right hand with both the line and the leader. Keep the loop open. Make a second overhand knot. Pull all four ends at the same time to tighten the knot.

Uni-Knot

A uni-knot is a tough-loop knot that tests at about 90 percent, and it will slip tight on a strike. Slip the loop open after landing a fish. The uni-knot will need to be retied after each fish if you're using light line. This is an excellent knot when using the new super braided lines.

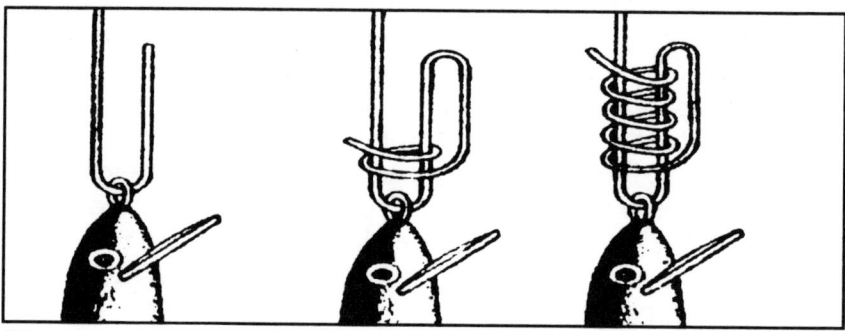

Hang a lure on the line as shown, pinching the main line and tag end with your thumb and forefinger about four inches above the lure. Leave six inches dangling at the tag end. Make three or four wraps around the parallel lines. Tighten the knot against the lure or on the main line to form a loop. Don't trim the tag too close.

Bow Knot

The bow knot is frequently used on crankbaits that are being run without a snap. It ties a firm loop that al-

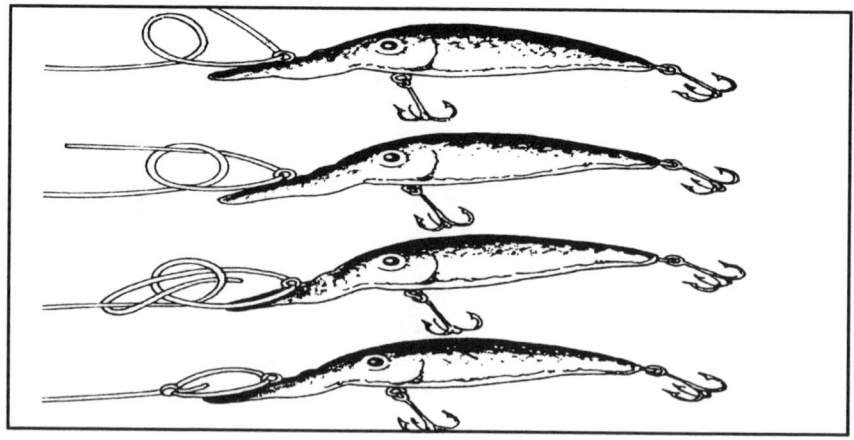

lows maximum movement, yet it doesn't restrict the crankbaits action.

Trilene Knot

The Trilene knot is the "bread and butter" knot. It's useful for most walleye tackle systems including snells, snaps, lures, swivels, and bottom bouncers.

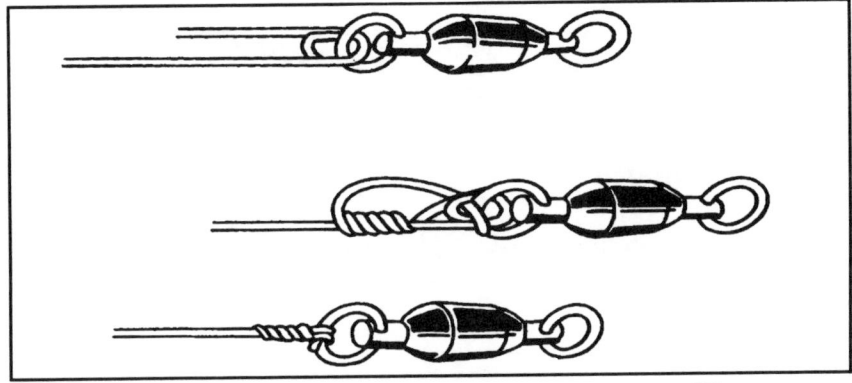

First, put two wraps through the connection. Then wrap four times or better for 15-pound test or better, use five wraps for lighter line.

Loop Knot

The loop knot is the "in the dark knot." It's easy to tie by feel or when your fingers are cold. The loop knot will offer the same characteristics as the bow line knot.

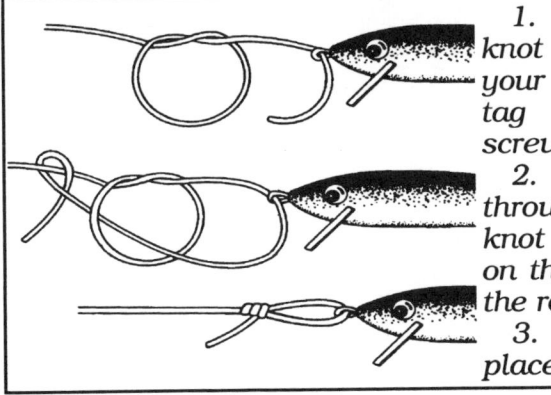

1. Tie an overhand knot near the end of your main line. Run the tag end through the screw eye.
2. Run the tag end through the overhand knot and tie a half-hitch on the main line nearest the rod.
3. Tighten the loop in place.

Nail Knot

The nail knot shines when connecting erratic line diameters, such as a monofilament leader to lead core line. The nail creates a small flat knot that can be easily reeled through the rod eyes and into the reel.

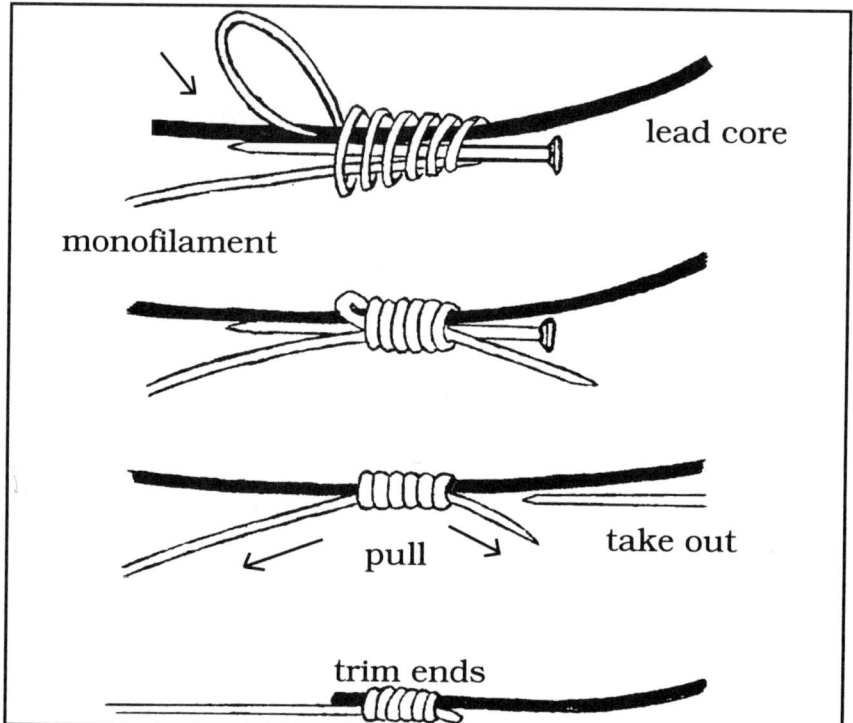

WHAT SIZE OR COLOR OF HOOKS DO I NEED?

There's nothing magic about choosing the right hooks. Simply select the hook that can do the job. The hard part is identifying the job. The job isn't as simple as just hooking a fish. When it comes to walleyes, it's hooking a fish with a large, bony mouth full of teeth. Now that you have defined the job, open your tackle box and throw away all those little, tiny hooks!

TROUBLE-SHOOTING TIP

Small Hooks?
There's only one reason to use a small hook, so it will fit into a small fish's mouth.

The smaller hook rule for walleyes has nothing to do with hooking them. Small hooks are merely a tool for a particular presentation, Lindy rigging. Lindy rigging is a presentation where a small hook is inserted into live bait. Once the fish picks the bait up, free line is given so the fish can swim off and swallow the bait along with the smaller hook. After the bait is swallowed, you can set the hook. The smaller hook will do an excellent job of penetrating into the stomach lining or throat. For this presentation, small hooks are perfect; they are easy for the fish to swallow and be hooked.

Smaller hooks are great for Lindy rigging, but when you consider other presentations such as jigs, bottom bouncers or crankbaits, big hooks are the rule. BIG, SHARP hooks! Not only do they need to be big and sharp, but there are other characteristics required from a hook to perform best for each presentation. Let's look

TROUBLE-SHOOTING TIP

If Hooks Could Talk

When you look at hook sizes, styles, and an array of colors that range from fluorescent to chrome to gold, a huge selection is offered. But if a hook could talk, it would say, "I'd rather be sharp than pretty." Sharp hooks catch fish, color doesn't.

at the five characteristics you should consider when selecting a hook. Three of these apply to all presentations and are a must for all walleye hooks:

1) The first and foremost characteristic for any hook of any type is to be very sharp!

2) A hook should have a wide gap. Remember, walleyes have a large, hard mouth with many teeth.

3) You need strong tips that won't fold over or break when it snags on logs or rocks. Flexibility and wire diameter, the remaining two characteristics, depend on the presentation. Let me address each presentation.

Jigging

The first thing I look for in a jig hook is a wide gap (the distance between the shank and the point). Many times, particularly with small jigs, the gap is so narrow and the hook point too close to the jig head that they are almost fish-proof. Even on the lightest jig, I use a #1 or #2 hook.

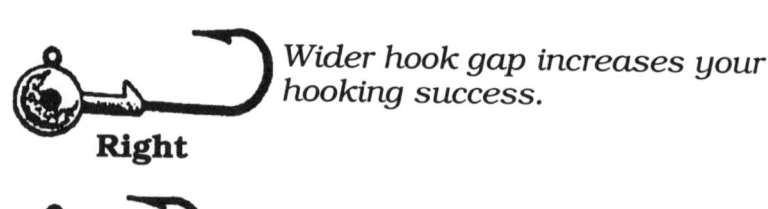

Wider hook gap increases your hooking success.

Right

Hook point too close to eye.

Wrong

Next, check the flexibility. The ideal jig hook is one that will straighten out and pull free from snags without breaking six-pound test line. It's easier and quicker to simply bend your jig hook back into position than to tie a new one, especially with bad light, cold fingers, or if you're like me and wear glasses.

Next, I check the hook's point not just for sharpness but for strength. Many of the super sharp hooks have points so fine that the tip of the point breaks or rolls over easily. Look for hooks with a meaty point that will stand some abuse. You can always re-sharpen the hook.

Rigging

If I intended to keep each fish I catch on a rig, I'd select a small hook. My choice for hooks with this presentation is a #4 light wire Fang hook made by Quick Change Systems. Small hooks are easy for walleyes to swallow and are very effective at hooking. If fish are to be released, don't use small hooks and allow the fish to swallow them. No matter how much care is taken in releasing these fish, a gut-hooked fish has a slim chance for survival.

If you're culling small fish or releasing larger ones, choose big hooks and a quick strike method of rigging that will hook the walleye in the mouth, rather than the gullet or throat. For this type of rigging, use a #1 or #2 Aberdeen hook. Choose the lightest wire hook that has the same characteristics of wide gaps and flexibility as your jigging hooks.

Bottom Bouncer

If I'm using a bottom bouncer and straight hook set-up (a four to six feet leader with a single hook for live bait), I'll use the exact same hook as for the quick strike rigging. Choose a #1 or #2 light wire Aberdeen hook.

For bottom bouncers and spinners (worm harnesses), strength is a key factor in hook selection. A bottom bouncer and spinner system is generally tied with 15 to 20-pound test line. There are two reasons for this heavy line. The first reason is that it's a presentation that doesn't have to deal with finesse, so a major advantage of strength can be applied. Stronger line also allows you to pull free from more snags thus saving some tackle. The second reason for the stronger line is clevis wear. The continuous rotating of the spinner blade and clevis will quickly wear through a lighter line. Heavy line means heavy hooks. My choice for bottom bouncers and spinners is a #2 fang hook with an up-turned eye.

Crankbaits

Hook choices for crankbaits are very simple, replace them all. Remove the factory hooks and replace them with a good quality hook of the exact same size. I replace all my hooks with Excalibur rotating treble hooks. I wouldn't consider another hook style. Excaliburs give me a huge hooking advantage over conventional treble hooks. Designed with a counter-rotating angle in each hook bend, each of the two free points travel counter clockwise once contact is made with one point. This movement of hook points results in at least one other point coming into contact with a striking fish. Although these hooks are a little higher in price, they are well worth it.

I have explained my reasons for selecting certain hooks. You may use different hooks and that's fine, but always remember to select the best tool to do the job.

As for the second part of this question: "What color do you need?" Who cares? Fish don't.

WHAT'S A CRANKBAIT?

I know crankbaits catches a great amount of fish. I know they seem to catch bigger fish. And, one thing I know for sure: "I know the exact depth 200 different crankbaits will run trolling or casting."

I wrote a book called <u>Crankbaits</u> and published a "Crankbait Depth Guide and Calculator" (a guide that lists the exact depths of 200 different crankbaits when trolled or cast on five different line sizes), but when asked, "What's a crankbait?" I think back to what my grandfather used to call "plugs." My dad called them "lures." Now we call the same things "crankbaits."

I needed help on this one, so I contacted my good buddy Joe Hughes. Joe's in charge of public relations for PRADCO. They manufacture several different lines of crankbaits including the Bomber, Rebel, Heddon and Cotton Cordell, which is also the manufacturer of the Wally Diver. If anyone can tell you exactly what a crankbait is, Joe can.

Most anglers, even those with little experience, know exactly what a crankbait is. It's a plug that one casts or trolls and, as the lure is being retrieved, it dives and wobbles.

The key to utilizing this popular fishing tool is to understand the characteristics inherent in each individual crankbait. Simply stated, each crankbait exhibits eight major characteristics, and the more you know about each one of these, the more proficient you will be with crankbaits.

The following list represents crankbait's characteristics, explanations, and general order of importance. During varying times and conditions, certain characteristics may move higher on the list, becoming a major factor in

the fish-catching ability of the specific lure chosen. They are:
1. Depth
2. Speed
3. Action
4. Buoyancy
5. Color
6. Sound
7. Size
8. Shape

If you take the time to learn the characteristics of each crankbait you own, you'll be in a much better position to make those quick decisions that may positively affect your fishing success.

The first thing to learn about any crankbait is the **depth** it runs. Knowing the depth where the fish are and selecting a lure that runs at that depth is critical. You also need to understand how external factors such as the length of your cast and the diameter of your fishing line will affect the depth each lure can attain.

Author Mike McClelland has taken much of the guesswork out of the exercise in depth. His "Crankbait Depth Chart" takes the more popular cranks and gives you the depth information under different casting/trolling distances as well as different diameters of line. For the anglers wishing to achieve the most out of every crankbait they own, Mike's publication is a must.

Speed is one of the hardest characteristics to initially grasp. When one learns how the speed of retrieving or trolling affects lure depth, its importance as a characteristic is easily understood. The most important thing to remember is that the faster a crankbait moves through the water, the more shallow that lure will run. For crankbait casters, this means the "retrieval" ratio on the reel is the first piece of information you need to learn. Knowing the speed limitations of the lures you own and use is very important.

Once you've mastered the depth and speed characteristics of your crankbaits, you may begin to learn how selecting other characteristics can help build a game plan that will increase success with lures while on the water.

Certain characteristics such as **buoyancy** are much more important to casters. Through physical contact with their lure, casters create unique lure **actions** by utilizing certain buoyancy characteristics.

Learning the **sound** characteristics of each lure is also important. Some lures have internal rattles that create a distinctive frequency and amplitude underwater. However, even without rattles, hook noise and water dis-

placement create different yet receivable vibrations underwater.

*Experimentation with lure **size** should lead to the conclusion that the smaller the lure, the more strikes; however, these added strikes won't necessarily come from the targeted species.*

***Shape**, especially in clear water, can be of extreme importance. Lures that represent some type of familiar forage fish may be very productive especially when combined with an erratic action that signals distress.*

***Color** is the most diversified choice you have in a lure characteristic. Don't be fooled by what the human eye can see and relate to under water. Remember, predator fish have evolved over millions of year in an underwater environment. Scientific studies have proven that fish see and relate to different colors, but we really can only imagine how well they see within their own environment.*

Hopefully, you are impressed with the complex nature of what most anglers feel is a simple lure to fish, the crankbait. Like most anything else, the more you know about them and their characteristics, the more valuable tool crankbaits will become.

I'm not only impressed with Joe's knowledge, but now I know the characteristics of crankbaits. I do think Joe left something out - crankbaits aren't magic! Firstly, you have to locate fish (if there are no fish, you can't catch them, no matter what crankbait you use). Secondly, fine tune your presentations to allow fish to take your bait. If they can't get the bait into their mouths, you can't catch them. When you can solve these two steps, then consider all the characteristics of different crankbaits. Incorporate this with my "Crankbait Depth Guide," and your success is going to increase.

WHAT'S A BOTTOM BOUNCER?

The bottom bouncer was developed in the early 1970's by a Missouri River fisherman from the Pierre, South Dakota, area. It fit the needs of the Dakota anglers who had been frustrated with the lake's snaggy structures and their traditional Wolf River Rigs tendency to find them. The Wolf River Rig is a three-way swivel with a drop sinker that was used for the same purpose as a bottom bouncer; to present a bait a foot off the bottom. By replacing the three-way swivel and drop sinker with a stiff wire and a weight molded in the center, the bottom bouncer made it possible to have a snag free contact with the bottom.

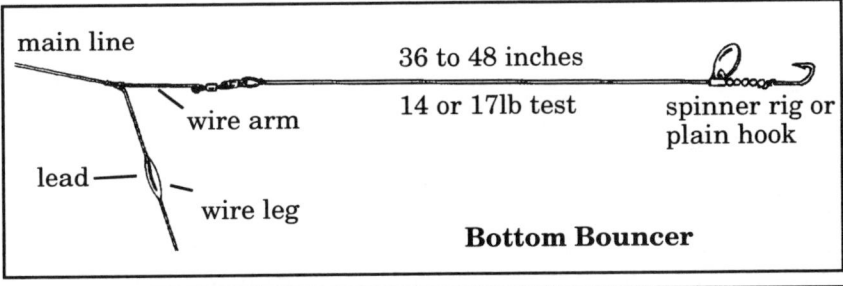

Bottom Bouncer

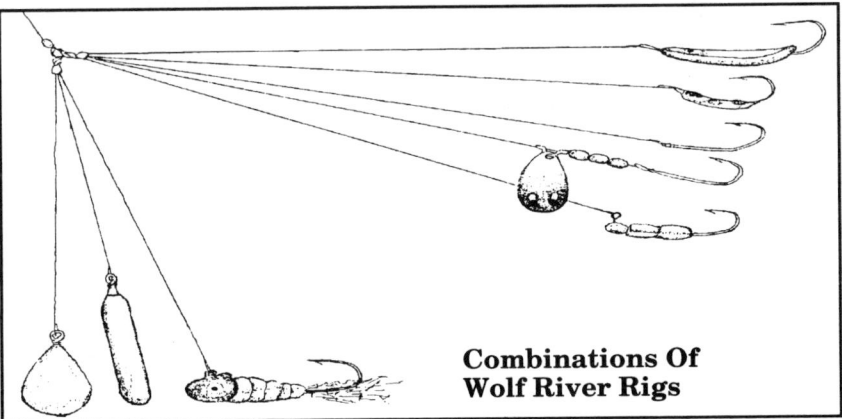

Combinations Of Wolf River Rigs

> ## TROUBLE-SHOOTING TIP
> ### A Bottom Bouncer Can't Be Fished Wrong
> The bottom bouncers effectiveness is multiplied by the fact that you don't have to be a professional fishermen to catch fish with it. A kid can out-fish a pro. It's a system that really can't be fished wrong.

For years the bottom bouncer was the walleye tackle mainstay in the Dakotas. When introduced to out-of-state fishermen, jaws would drop in disbelief and the statement would be: "What a crude way to fish; there must be a better way." After trying "Dakota" tactics, they soon fell into the ranks of the bottom bouncer fishermen.

The bottom bouncer was manufactured in garages and marketed in South Dakota until 1981 when Lindy Little Joe produced a model called the Bottom Cruiser. Today's bottom bouncer has been refined even further with a system called Lite Bite, marketed by Quick Change Systems. The Lite Bite has an added ability for the weight to slip which will allow you to feed line to finicky fish while still having snag-free benefits of the bottom bouncer.

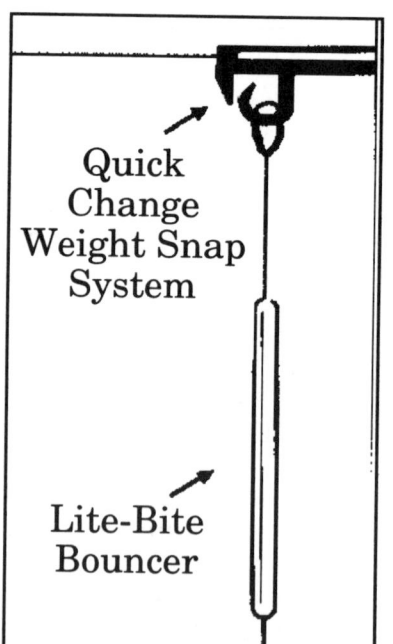

Quick Change Weight Snap System

Lite-Bite Bouncer

The Lite Bite by Quick Change Systems is the advancement of the bottom bouncer. Lite Bites can be fished like a bottom bouncer and a Lindy rig at the same time. With the Quick Change snap, the Lite Bite's weights can be changed at any time.

QUESTION 20 — WHAT'S A BOTTOM BOUNCER?

The bottom bouncer was definitely a well kept secret until the mid-1980's when the Manufacturers Walleye Council created the first walleye fishing circuit. This circuit drew excellent walleye anglers from all over the country to specific locations where they could share tactics and knowledge. Prior to this, walleye fishing knowledge had been limited to a few basic tactics that were passed from Father to Son. The tournament circuits created *the* events and *the* atmosphere for a blend of knowledge from across the country.

Bob Propst, Sr., and I had the privilege of introducing the first bottom bouncer to the tournament scene. The initial tournament on the trail was in Minnesota on Lake Mille Lacs, and naturally we thought bottom bouncers would work and be accepted anywhere. While pre-fishing on the first day, we stopped at one of the resorts for some information and a few sodas. As we returned to the dock, we saw a local guide we had met earlier standing with a group of his buddies staring into our boat and chuckling. "Hi fella's," my partner Bob said. "What's so funny?" As the guide wiped the tears of laughter from his eyes, he asked, "What's that you got hanging on the end of your rod?" Bob replied, "It's called a bottom bouncer." The next question the guide asked was typical, "What do you do with it?" Bob undauntedly answered, "We catch walleyes with it." As the questioners roared with laughter, the guide looked at us and stated, "Our walleyes in Minnesota have too much fi-

---

TROUBLE-SHOOTING TIP

Only One Rule

There is only one rule when fishing with bottom bouncers - let out just enough line to touch bottom. If there is too much line out, the bottom bouncer falls over and will snag or drag flat on the bottom. Fish it with the attitude that you're using it to keep track of the bottom. Lift it up and then drop it, again and again.

nesse to eat something like that." Well, it's a good thing we didn't listen. The bottom bouncer is now one of the most popular tactics used on Mille Lacs, just like everywhere else. (By the way, the guide who was laughing at our bottom bouncer isn't laughing anymore - he's won over $50,000 on the P.W.T. circuit using it.)

In the past 10 years, the bottom bouncer has become one of the most valuable tools among professional walleye fishermen. Whether in rivers, lakes or reservoirs, the bottom bouncer is an effective presentation to catch walleyes on structure.

There are three reasons the bottom bouncer is so effective:

1) You don't have to be a professional fishermen to catch fish with it. The weekend angler will catch just as many fish as the avid walleye "warrior," and it doesn't take years of light line experience or hundreds of dollars of equipment. It's a very basic system that you really can't fish wrong.

2) The bottom bouncer is nearly snag-free. Its design is the key. It has a weight molded onto the middle of a stainless steel wire with a wire arm that forms a loop and attaches to a leader at the top. By running your bottom bouncer at a 45-degree angle with just enough line out to touch bottom, you can fish free of most rocks and snags. Remember, a rough bottom holds many fish, but it also eliminates some fishing methods such as jigs and Lindy Rigs.

3) The bottom bouncers can be fished from 50 to 10 feet and then back to 50 feet. The bottom line is simple. The bottom bouncer presents a bait approximately one foot off the bottom at any depth, and that's the WALLEYE ZONE!

HOW DO YOU CHOOSE THE BEST LIVE BAIT?

Choose a live bait for convenience and how it'll be used. Choose a live bait not by what you think a walleye *wants* to eat, but by what you think he *should* be eating. How could a walleye know that he wants to eat a nightcrawler? He's never seen one before, and it's not his natural food. Granted, some nightcrawlers may be washed into the system, but they're generally savored by panfish and rough fish long before a walleye ever takes a "whack" at them. The only thing *natural* about a nightcrawler in 20 feet of water is that he is dead, drowned, and probably lying limp and lifeless on the bottom.

How about leeches? Although an excellent bait, leeches aren't a natural bait either. They don't live where walleyes do. The first leech a walleye sees will surely have a hook in it.

To choose the right live bait you must forget about any connection to the word "natural." Don't give a walleye credit for picking or choosing what he wants to eat; he's not out hunting for a nightcrawler just because he had one yesterday that tasted good. Also ignore your calendar. There's no such thing as walleyes wanting to eat minnows in the spring, nightcrawlers starting about May 1, and leeches beginning around June 15. Walleyes don't think, make choices or decisions, and they don't have a calendar!

TROUBLE-SHOOTING TIP
Live Bait Selection
Fresh and lively are the key things to look for when selecting live bait, regardless of what *you* choose.

There are three considerations I use when selecting live bait:

1) The foremost consideration and impact on your success is to always choose the freshest and liveliest bait. Life and movement are keys to live bait success. Change your live bait frequently; don't use it until the bait is dead.

2) Convenience is the real reason for live bait selection. Minnows are a good example. We know walleyes eat minnows year-around, but we don't use them in July and August. Why? It's very simple: they're not convenient. By the time you buy minnows and get them back to the boat at that time of year, they may be all dead! If you do manage to keep them alive long enough to use as bait, they require constant maintenance. It's much wiser to select a bait such as leeches that require minimum maintenance on hot summer days.

3) Another important consideration when choosing live bait is how it will be used. Jig fishing provides a good example. (When casting a jig, avoid minnows as you may be constantly casting off the minnow and fishing without any live bait.) Choose a bait that's tough and durable; half a nightcrawler works well. A crawler is good for nearly a hundred casts or until a fish is caught.

A nightcrawler is the only choice for bottom bouncer fishing. Why? If I miss a fish, I have a much better chance that he only snatched half the bait. With a leech or minnow the odds improve in the fish's favor.

If Lindy rigging, a leech is the answer. A leech is durable and can live and swim for hours. The leech's continuous action is very important since Lindy rigging depends on the bait to provide the action from its movement.

These are some of the real reasons for your choice with live bait: Consider them on your next fishing trip. Remember, adapt the bait to the type of rig you are fishing with.

Part III

WHERE YOU NEED TO GO

84 WALLEYE TROUBLE-SHOOTING

A look at a walleye from a minnows' point of view!

WHAT'S THE FASTEST WAY TO LOCATE WALLEYES?

One of the most difficult problems anglers face, if not the single, most difficult problem, is *locating* walleyes. Success rate climbs tremendously once the fish are found. Trying to determine where to start on any given day is often the problem.

Communication is the key. Some call it "pre-fishing." It's the first step in locating walleyes and probably the most overlooked. Pre-fishing information is what you need to know before you arrive at your destination. Lake Oahe in South Dakota is a good example. So many times I see anglers who are unfamiliar with the Dakota waters pull up to the lake without any idea of where to begin. They don't realize that the Dakota reservoirs are huge and contain thousands of miles of shoreline. (Lake Oahe alone has 2,300 miles of shoreline.) That means the active bite may be a hundred miles away.

To reach the area of the lake that has the "hot" bite is half the battle. For this information you can rely heavily on baitshops as a solid source, but not just one! Check as many as you can. Baitshops are constantly on top of the activity. They know what's happening, what's hot and what's not. They're glad to relay this information to you, and you should take advantage of it. It's been my experience that people don't give baitshops enough credibility for their information. Aside from selling bait and tackle, their business depends on giving you good information on hot-spots and hot tackle.

Remember, communication is the key to locating walleyes, whether it is at the baitshop, the boat ramps or fishing club meetings. You'll find out quickly that the more you talk, the better you fish; the better you fish, the more you talk.

South Dakota Tourism Photo

Smiling is the secret to communication and better fishing information.

QUESTION 22 — WHAT'S THE FASTEST WAY TO LOCATE WALLEYES?

TROUBLE-SHOOTING TIP

Communication:
The Key To Catching More Walleyes

First, understand that walleyes aren't hard to catch; they're hard to find. Believe me, you don't have enough fishing time in your life to do all the things that could be and should be tried even on one lake, let alone taking on new waters.

Share the task by joining a fishing club. Visit with anglers on the water, stop at the bait shops rather than the "quick" shop. They both have ice and soda, but only the bait shops have the latest, most up-to-date fishing information. Be sure to visit with any walleye angler who's just been fishing. Simply ask, "Did you have any luck?" I know you already do this, but when he tells you, "No," you may say, "Too bad" and go about your business. Not me. I continue the conversation. I want to know exactly where he was and why he didn't catch anything. I don't want to repeat his failure.

Be friendly, communicate and smile, you'll catch more fish and have more fun.

Bob Propst, Jr. - Communicating!

TROUBLE-SHOOTING TIP

Lake Maps

When you visit a new area to fish, always stop at the baitshops - all of the baitshops! Buy a map of the lake from each, even though it's the same map. (These maps are only valuable if purchased from *that* store). Lay the map on the counter and ask the baitshop owner if there is anything about the lake that's not on the map. (I've never met a baitshop owner that didn't know more about the lake then the guy that made the map). Once he gets his pencil out, you'll then get the valuable information that isn't on the map such as weedlines, small rock piles, hard and soft bottoms. Most of all you'll find out where they caught 'em yesterday!

By the time you gather this information from three or four baitshops, you'll have the most accurate and up-to-date information on the lake.

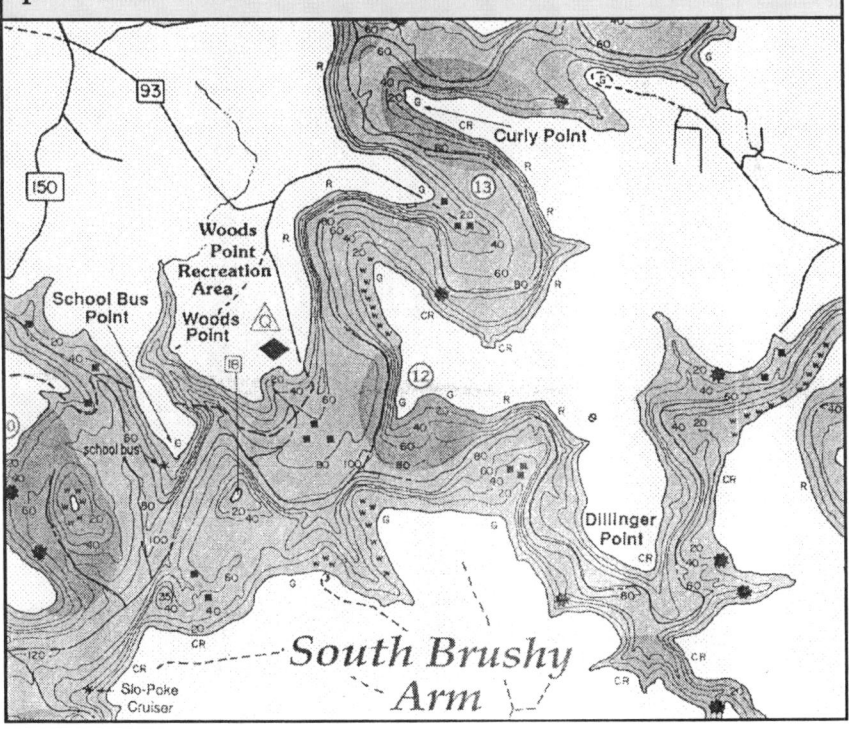

Author Mike McClelland with a nice Lake Oahe walleye.

HOW DO YOU LOCATE WALLEYES IN RESERVOIRS & LAKES?

Locating walleyes on big lakes and reservoirs is a major problem for the average angler; however, this problem can be easily solved by following in order a few simple steps:

Step One

First address the easiest fish to locate, the ones that are always right where they're supposed to be. Fish off the longest points and the fastest breaks on the flats. These areas can be seen with the naked eye or can be found with the aid of topographical maps. The points need to be checked first, and they need to be re-checked with your electronics.

Don't fish "memories" (last year's spots), particularly on reservoirs. These reservoirs change and can become whole new lakes with each new year. When 10 feet is added or subtracted from a body of water, an entirely new lake is created with new spots, new holding areas, new food shelves. The first thing to do is forget about the spots where you caught fish last year.

Use your electronics and your eyes to find new spots. Begin by checking where the fish should be which is from 10 to 30 feet off long points and underwater humps. Do this by "contour cutting," searching from 45 feet up to 10 feet, then back to 45, and up and down the

---

TROUBLE-SHOOTING TIP

Short Quote
The only thing I know for sure is this: "If there's no fish here, you can't catch 'em!"

92 WALLEYE TROUBLE-SHOOTING

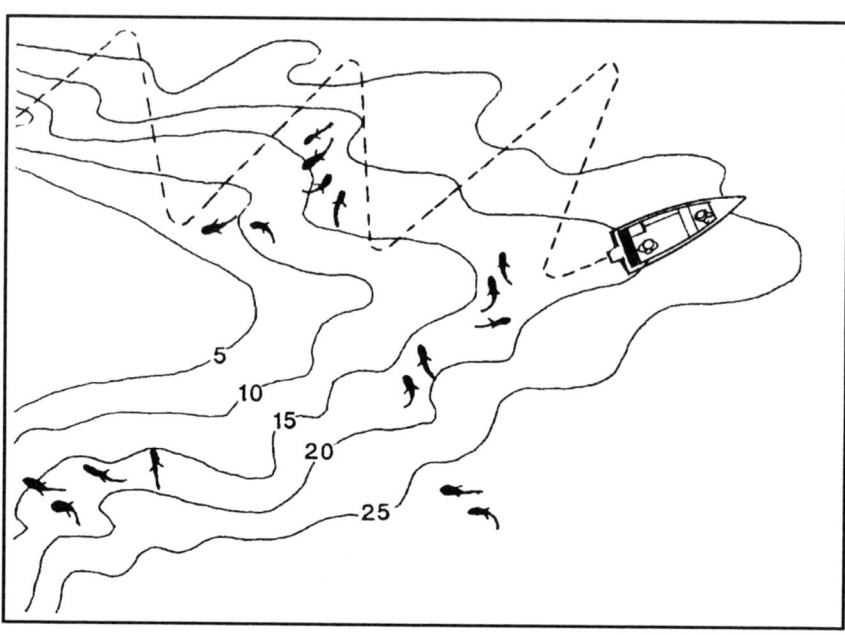

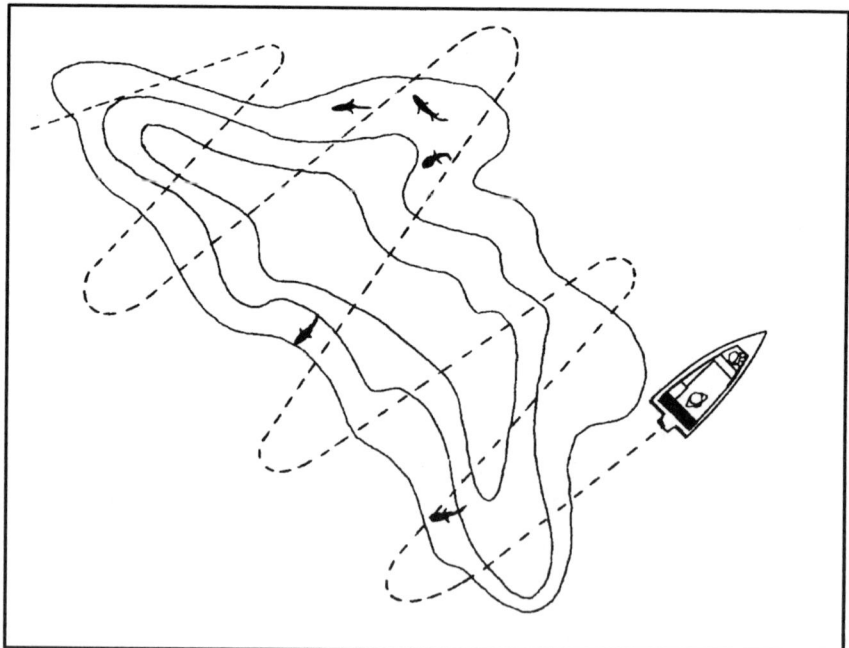

This is what contour-cutting looks like from an aerial-view.

breaks following the structure. What you're looking for is actual fish. If you don't mark fish, you simply don't fish there. If they're not there, move onto the next point. When you're looking for scattered fish between 10 and 40 feet of water, expect to only find a few. The number of fish isn't as important as the depth in which they're located. Perhaps you may only mark three fish on one point, but if those fish were all at 17 feet, that's a good place to start. Those fish are usually a good bet.

Many people expect to see many fish on their electronics. Two or three fish at a particular depth on my Humminbird Wide represents enough fish to make the effort worthwhile. Remember that you're seeing very little with your electronics, just a small circle below your boat. Don't try to work a specific fish, but work the specific depth.

Step Two

If the fish aren't found in the traditional, obvious places, check mid-range depths. Depths of five to 12 feet are the best choices. These mid-range depths have to be physically fished. You can't use your electronics to locate fish here because the cone angle of the transducer is too small. To fish mid-range depths, go with the high-percentage spots and use a method that covers a great deal of water quickly. Fast-moving presentations like trolling spinners or casting crankbaits work well. These shallow fish will be active, and they'll chase a bait. Try to work fast and cover as much water as possible in a short time.

If you don't find fish in mid-range depths after two or three tests, it's safe to assume that "nobody's home" today. You've eliminated that area, and it's time for the next step.

Step Three

Begin looking for fish directly in the shallow water it-

> ## TROUBLE-SHOOTING TIP
> ### Recognize Visual Aids
> The key to fishing shallow water is learning how to recognize the visual aids. Visual aids not only point out areas that you should be fishing, but more importantly, they also eliminate the vast majority of the shore line.

self, an ideal place to find aggressive, feeding walleyes. This water is up to five feet deep and should never be overlooked. Fish will move with the food, and much of the time that's in very shallow water. Again, this has to be physically fished, usually by casting.

Fortunately, with shallow water you have a great number of visual aids that eliminate most of the shoreline to locate active walleyes. Some of these visual aids are simple. Say you notice three or four boats working a long point on deeper, neutral fish that won't bite. It's a good bet that some of these fish could move up to feed between the boats and the bank. Throw a jig and minnow or crankbait up into the shallow water. The "hot" fish will pull away from the neutral fish further out and move into the shallow water to eat, much like the guy getting off the couch and heading for the refrigerator during a TV commercial. These fish will leave their comfort zone and move into the shallow water for food. It's a good high percentage choice.

Another visual aid for shallow water angling success is to avoid banks with a very slow taper such as a beach. Fish the banks with a "bumper" that drop abruptly for a foot or two. You'll often see rocks, responsible for the quick drops, along such shorelines. These are choice areas to try. Walleyes, without revealing their presence, can slip into these areas for easy feeding. Cast these areas with jigs or crankbaits. Remember, don't run the boat over them as walleyes "spook" easily in shallow water.

The final factor in shallow water choices involves

mudlines. Anytime you have waves rolling into a point or bar, you'll have a mudline with varying degrees of visibility. These spots need to be fished very shallowly. Never overlook the walleye's desire to get into shallow, muddy water to find food. Fish not only the mudline area where the dirty water meets the clean, but also fish the shallowest dirty water. Cast within a foot of the bank. The fish at times will be very, very shallow.

Step Four

If all has failed after trying steps one to three, face it, you're day may almost be shot. There's one more thing you can do, and that is to check the back of the bays. Rarely are all the backs of the bays explored, and often they can hold a tremendous walleye fishery. Don't overlook them!

Checking the back-bay areas is very simple and quick. First, choose the bigger bays, and go to the extreme end of these areas. Then come back to the first prevalent point in the bay. Fish just like you would on a shallow water point, casting your jigs or crankbaits into them. If vegetation exists be certain to work the edges with different presentations.

Try trolling crankbaits in five to 10 feet of water using your big engine. This method covers a tremendous amount of territory and lets you locate active fish quickly. It's also a method that can provide "hot action" from other species including northern pike, bass and panfish.

96 WALLEYE TROUBLE-SHOOTING

Bob Propst, Sr. - Professional guide, tournament fishermen, National Freshwater Fishing Hall Of Fame member, and grand master of fishing walleye in current.

WHAT ABOUT CURRENT?

More than 900,000 miles of river exist in the United States and nearly half of them harbor fishable populations of walleyes. Yet for some reason, a majority of walleye fishermen spend their time fishing lakes rather than on a stretch of current. Part of the reason might be a trend in the tackle industry. Bigger, lighter boats with more fuel-efficient motors and innovations such as trolling boards and global positioning systems (GPS), have combined to make fishing on large, open-water lakes relatively easy. These advances have greatly helped to unlock the expanding fisheries on places like Lake Erie, reservoirs in the West, Midwest and South and numerous large Canadian shield lakes.

The real revolution in walleye fishing has been provided by the field of electronics. Before electronics, midlake structures such as humps, reefs, flats, and submerged weedbeds were forgotten and overlooked. Today, fishermen can motor for hours by GPS coordinates to an underwater target.

On rivers visual aids can replace modern technology. "Keep it simple" is the best piece of advice for fishing a river. Instead of sensitive electronic equipment for reading activity *beneath* the surface, we need to be alert to what's going on *above* the surface of the water. It's a back-to-the-basics type of fishing, putting your ability into tune with the physical environment and not the sonar screen.

Common lake strategy won't net you many river fish either. River fishing isn't difficult, it's just different. Although the rule that location dictates presentation still applies, another ingredient must be considered - CURRENT!

Rivers are constantly changing, almost daily. Rarely do they stay the same depth or have the same water clarity for more than a short period of time. Rivers can change almost hourly in tail-water situations near large power-generating dams. They can also rise and drop by the foot during periods of moderate rainfall. The implications are obvious. You must stay on top of the fish. They change as often as the river itself.

Visual aids are the key. Obstructions such as wind dams, rocks, logs and pilings that reduce current and create deep water pockets in the river bed can be recognized by reading the ripples of the water. They're excellent places to begin your search, and you can read them like a book; the surface will be slack and bubbles will often break on the surface.

Sometimes the current direction may even reverse itself and become an eddy. Because most of the fish will be facing into the current, your lure must be pulled throughout the eddy from a number of different angles. It sounds elementary, but nine out of 10 fishermen make their casts from only one location on the river. Because of speed and direction, your bait is then presented to only a limited number of fish in a limited area.

TROUBLE-SHOOTING TIP

Fish Eddies From The Bank

River eddies are the most obvious and easiest to fish. Bank fishermen can have a distinct advantage in current. It's no big deal to flip a few casts at the cutting edge of the swirl, then move over and up to make another cast. In a short time, the entire eddy can be worked.

With many rivers lacking decent boat launches and having stretches of river that are not navigable; you'll quickly realize that a pair of waders has its rightful place in any serious river fishing game plan. With them you can also get out of the boat and fish some eddies from the shore easier than from the boat.

| QUESTION 24 | WHAT ABOUT CURRENT? | 99 |

Changing your location and the direction of your cast to cover all areas of the eddy increases your fish-catching odds.

What is the best presentation for rivers? Jigs are the hands-down winners for both bank and boat presentations. Fishing jigs in rivers, especially along swifter sections, creates a common predicament; the current swallows up the jig and puts a big belly, or slack, in your line. The net result is less feeling and even less control. To hurdle this obstacle, most anglers go to a heavier jig (3/8 or 1/2 ounce). This, of course, makes it difficult for a walleye to suck in the bait leading to short-hits and fewer fish. The solution is simple. From the banks perspective, always cast at an upstream angle and let the cur

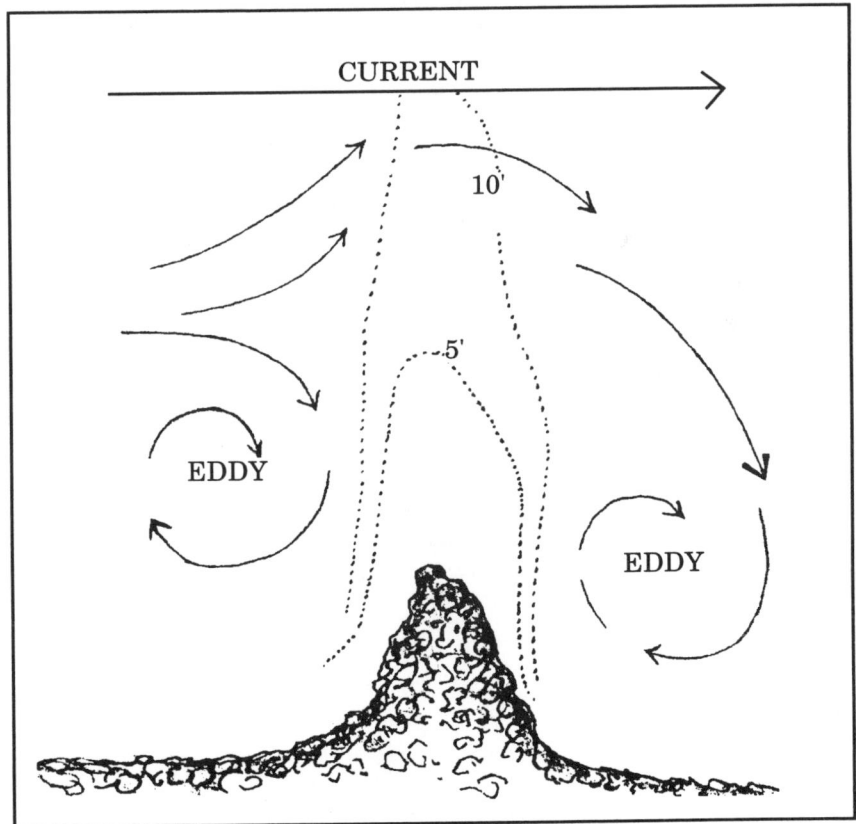

Watch and understand how eddies form.

rent present your jig with its natural downstream flow. When fishing from a boat, vertical jig whenever possible. This technique is simply done by controlling your drift with the current so that you pass directly over the fish as you bounce your jig off the bottom. This presentation allows you to use lighter jigs and also adds longevity to your presentation.

The key is to maintain your line in a vertical alignment at all times. When the current washes it to the left, you follow with the boat and rod tip to the left. Do the same for any other directional change. The best (and easiest) way to follow this procedure is with a bow mounted, Motor-Guide electric trolling motor. Put your transducer on the bottom shaft of the trolling motor to gain precise depth control and position.

As you chase your line, use your electric or kicker motor to keep the boat moving the same speed as the current, compensating for the wind against the boat. Always keep your line straight down. You'll find vertical jigging in current puts several important factors in your favor: 1) You'll always be sitting on top of the fish, 2) You'll have less snags as the result of added control, and 3) You'll have more free-fall time and more opportunity for a walleye to suck in the jig by increasing the height of the lift of the jig.

WHAT ABOUT PRE-SPAWN WALLEYES?

Walleyes spawn in rocky areas, instinctively seeking places that receive large amounts of wave action which does two things: oxygenates the eggs and keeps silt from covering them. These areas should be sought out in the early spring on lakes, reservoirs and rivers. The spawn begins when water temperatures reach 40 degrees and lasts until the water warms beyond 45 degrees. In the period leading up to the spawn, look around. You can use rip-rap, skull-sized rocks or other known spawning areas as your points of reference when searching for pre-spawners.

The quickest and easiest way to find spawning areas is to simply ask. Since walleyes spawn in the same locations year after year, someone will know where the spawn occurs. If you can't learn this information at local bait shops, contact the local conservation officer to put you on the right track.

The fish staging for the spawn, once the spawning area has been located, are easy to find with the help of a few simple rules. Begin at the spawning area as walleyes spawn in the same area year after year. Proceed from the spawning area and locate the closest 30-foot

---

TROUBLE-SHOOTING TIP

Big Bait Is Better

A key to catching walleyes durig the pre-spawn is to use big baits. The young of the year haven't hatched yet, so the main food for walleyes are the adult bait fish that have made it through the first year and are now fully grown. Add the biggest body you have to your jigs and cast or troll bigger crankbaits.

Bob Propst, Sr. - The man who wrote the rules to pre-spawn walleyes. During Bob Propst's 40 years of professional guiding, he had registered over 275 state Master Angler certificates for trophy walleyes exceeding 10 pounds, most by 1976. By 1976 he had caught and released over 600 walleyes that exceeded eight pounds. Pre-spawn walleyes accounted for over half of those fish.

QUESTION 25 WHAT ABOUT PRE-SPAWN WALLEYES?

level of water on the flattest bottom possible. Whether this depth is found in the backs of bays or the bottom of the lake, 30 feet is the key. If the lake doesn't have 30 feet of water, move to the closest, deepest part of the lake and begin looking there.

The fish can be easily found and are unmistakable. On your electronics, they'll mark as big hooks a foot or two off the bottom. It may not be on a red-hot bite, so fish them with confidence and big baits. Eventually a few will bite and two or three fish on any pre-spawn day is considered a great day.

The best method for taking pre-spawn fish is either Lindy rigging a large minnow four to six inches long or vertical jigging with a 1/4 ounce to 3/8 ounce jig using a large rubber body and a big minnow. My preference is both presentations at the same time.

TROUBLE-SHOOTING TIP

Slow Is The Key

Once you've located fish with electronics, remember fishing slow is the key. For jigging or rigging, you can't go too slow. Use your bow mount electric motor on the slowest speed. The slightest breeze will push you fast enough. Use a sea anchor to slow you even more.

Once you have located the fish, move your boat to the up-wind side and drift through them as slowly as possible. Let the Lindy rig trail 75 to 100 feet behind the boat and set the rod in a rod holder. Always keep an eye on the Lindy rig rod. When a hit is made, open the bail and give the fish a good deal of line and time before setting the hook.

When the Lindy rig rod is in its holder, vertically jig with the other rod. Jigging is easy - simply bounce the jig off the bottom, keeping it as close to vertical as possible. Unlike the Lindy rig, set the hook as soon as you feel a hit. For that matter, set the hook as soon as you *think* you feel a hit.

Al Linder holds up a nice male walleye taken off rip-rap along a dam during the spawn.

WHEN & WHERE DO WALLEYES SPAWN?

Walleyes spawn in water from one foot to over 20 feet deep. Rocky and gravel covered shorelines are the most typical spawning sites; however, if habitat is lacking walleyes will also spawn on sand and in other less desirable areas. An abundance of broken rocks and gravel in water three to 10 feet deep will normally attract the largest concentrations of fish.

TROUBLE-SHOOTING TIP

Water Temperature

In the spring, ignoring water temperature can be a costly mistake. Since walleyes spawn in the same places every year at predictable temperature levels, it is a simple matter to determine where the fish are in their spawning cycle. You can tell by temperature if the fish are close to spawning (pre-spawn) in the middle of it, or finished (post-spawn). This information, in turn, gives you a general idea of where the fish will be.

Reservoirs

Reservoir walleyes typically migrate to the upstream end of an impoundment to spawn. In large reservoirs, such as those along the Missouri River, walleyes have been known to travel 100 plus miles to reach prime spawning sites. Fisheries' biologists have tracked walleyes tagged with radio telemetry transmitters from one end of Lake Oahe in South Dakota to the other. Although this long distance may be an isolated incident, walleyes are nomadic creatures that won't hesitate to migrate many miles to find suitable spawning habitat.

106 **WALLEYE TROUBLE-SHOOTING**

Rod length is the key to trolling rip-rap during the spawn.

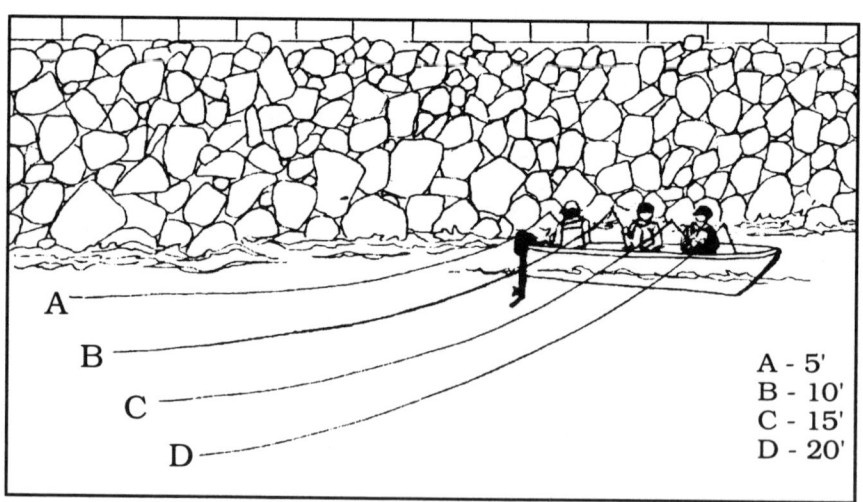

Trolling the rip-rap face of the dam with lures running from shallow to deep pin-points the exact depth. Different lures and rod lengths are critical here.

QUESTION 26 WHEN & WHERE DO WALLEYES SPAWN?

Rip-rap shorelines near the dams are often prime spawning areas. Trolling crankbaits along this rip-rap edge can prove absolutely deadly on big fish. The best action usually takes place after dark and continues until about midnight.

Although many walleyes prefer to spawn just downstream from dams, the rocky shorelines and tributary streams also attract spawn-laden fish. Not all the fish spawn at the same time or in the same places. This is Mother Nature's way of ensuring that an entire "year class," those particular fish that are born each year, isn't destroyed by floods or other natural disasters.

Rivers

Walleyes that spawn in rivers are the most predictable of all. Clearly, 99 percent of the fish that enter the river to spawn will physically swim as far as they possibly can before stopping to deposit their eggs. Low head dams, waterfalls, or natural and man-made diversions,

---

TROUBLE-SHOOTING TIP

Peak Walleye Activity

Your best chances to catch a spawning walleye are definitely between dark and midnight. The telemetry studies we've reviewed show a definite trend with the majority of the fish arriving just at dark and spawning until about midnight.

We've also found that fish spawn primarily for about four hours. One fish might pull in and spawn for four hours and be done all in one night. Another may come four different nights and spawn an hour each night. In between these nightly visits, she'll make large movements, sometimes up to five miles as the staging areas can be a long way away from the actual spawning bed. Again, a key to big walleye success during pre-spawn: "Be there at dark and don't stay any later than midnight."

usually stop the upstream movement of fish and often cause the concentration of tremendous numbers of big fish in amazingly small areas. At times, the walleyes will be so thick you can feel your lure bouncing off the backs of the fish. Fishing under these conditions can be easy and rewarding.

Natural Lakes

Walleyes that spawn in natural lakes are often the last fish of the season to deposit their eggs. It usually takes a week or two longer for the sun to warm these large inland lakes to the magical 40 to 45 degree spawning temperature that walleyes prefer.

Troll the spawning areas with shallow diving crankbaits such as a Rebel Minnow or floating Rattlin' Rogues. Trolling is by far the most effective method I have found for taking spawning walleyes along rip-rap or rocky shores. Long-lining crankbaits with eight-pound test line will produce the best results. Troll at a fairly brisk pace and use a combination of long and short rods to stair-step lure depths to match the angle of the structure. This will keep all your baits in the fish zone.

Set the rods on the side of the boat closest to the rip-rap. Use a long rod (eight to nine-foot) to reach out from the boat and present the crankbait along the edge of the rocks. A shallow diving Rebel Minnow is the ideal lure for the outside rod. The Rebel Minnow only dives two to three feet, but that is enough to keep the lure ticking the stones near shore. Next, set up a shorter rod with a slightly deeper diving lure like the Rattlin' Rogue. Set an even shorter third rod with an even deeper diving bait such as a Wally Diver. By following this procedure, you'll effectively cover the sloping rip-rap edges.

HOW DO YOU CATCH WALLEYES AFTER THE SPAWN?

After spawning is completed, predicting the whereabouts of big, trophy-sized walleyes can be very difficult. Post-spawn walleyes are going to be anywhere they can find something to eat. So you guessed it - food is the key.

After spawning, the accepted opinion is that walleyes go through a recuperation period that lasts 10 days or so during which the walleyes refuse to bite. This is not true. After spawning, the females immediately begin to slowly meander in the direction of their summer haunts. Males often can still be found in the spawning area and provide fishermen some great action until they eventually leave. The problem is many fishermen don't leave with the fish. Anglers tend to stay in the same area where they've been consistently catching fish, instead of accepting the fact that the fish have moved on. Many anglers think the fish are still there resting and recuperating from the work of the spawn and just aren't biting. Time for a wake up! Those fish have gone back to their summer habits and are eating like machines.

If you can find the fish right after the spawn, you'll catch them. The period right after the spawn, ranging into May and June is usually the best time of the year for walleye success. If a walleye needs to recuperate from the spawn, they do it by eating. Most of the food they find at this time of the year will be adult baitfish and panfish found in the shallows where they are taking their turn at the spawn.

110 WALLEYE TROUBLE-SHOOTING

TROUBLE-SHOOTING TIP

Post-Spawn Fish

The key to Post-Spawn fish is slow bait presentations - very, very slow. You have to remember that these fish are in cold water. They are very lethargic and slow moving, and they're not aggressively chasing food. But if you have a juicy tidbit that's available and give them time to react to it, these fish will hit. Don't expect a walleye boom. When fishing post-spawn fish and particularly big fish, three or less fish is a great day on anybody's lake.

QUESTION 27 **HOW DO YOU CATCH WALLEYES AFTER THE SPAWN?**

RIVERS

Rivers may be categorized into two different groups: 1) rivers where walleyes live in natural lakes during most of the year and their tributary streams where walleye spawn in the spring, and 2) rivers that maintain constant walleye populations throughout the year.

Walleyes that spawn in tributary streams or bays are much easier to locate in the weeks following the spawn. Although the majority of the largest walleyes leave the river immediately after spawning, a significant number of fish remain in the river to feed. Those fish migrating downstream to the main lake area of a reservoir often hold near the stream's mouth for several weeks to ambush baitfish that are entering the river to spawn.

The second group of river spawning walleyes include those fish that live in major river systems year-around. These fish are located fairly easily by checking depths of 10 to 20 feet using your electronics. The key is to consider any fish you see to be a walleye. Rivers including the Mississippi, Illinois and Missouri hold fish all year long. In the spring, those fish that migrate upstream often must pass through several locks and dams to reach the best spawning habitat. After spawning, the fish slowly drop back to the lower ends of the river pools where the current slows and food is concentrated. Any site along the way that concentrates baitfish is likely to attract walleyes. Shallow rip-rap shorelines and creek mouths are great places to begin looking.

LAKES AND RESERVOIRS

Predicting where the post-spawn walleyes are (in lakes and reservoirs) isn't easy. The fish are moving in every direction and wander constantly in search of food.

In the spring, ignoring water temperature can be a costly mistake. Since walleyes spawn in the same places every year and at predictable temperature levels, it is simply a matter of determining where the fish are in

Good boat control and patience is the key to Mike Theyerl's post-spawn success.

QUESTION 27 **HOW DO YOU CATCH WALLEYES** 113
AFTER THE SPAWN?

their spawning cycle. You can actually tell, by degrees, if the fish are close to spawning (pre-spawn), in the middle of it, or finished (post-spawn). This, in turn, will give you a general idea where the fish will be. It's really not as complicated as it may appear.

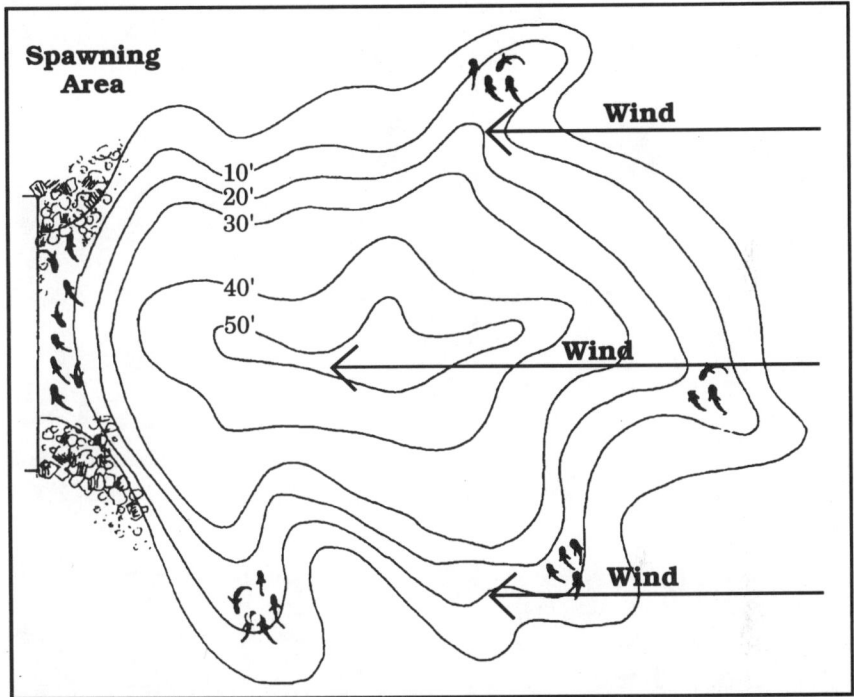

Early season fish in reservoirs will be drawn to shallow bays from which wind is flowing. Start with the major bays closest to the spawning area.

If the water temperature has been close to 50 degrees, you can assume the fish are gone from the spawning area. You can count on this year in and year out. To locate these fish, begin by searching for the warmest water. If the system has large bays, check the shallow end of the bays where the wind is blowing out. These will be the warmest bays. If the system you're fishing doesn't have big, shallow bays that warm quickly, remember that warmer water is the key. A shallow

Post-spawn fish in shallow water won the author the 1990 PWT tournament at Lake Oahe.

long point or a slowly tapering bank will warm more quickly. This warmer water will attract baitfish that bring with them the walleyes.

When I won the 1990 Cabala's/In-Fishermen Professional Walleye Trail Tournament on Lake Oahe in Mobridge, SD, the second week of May, I and the other contestants experienced weather that ranged from snowstorms to temperatures in the 80's. The big females had moved out of the spawning areas to post-spawn locations for the summer. With the absence of shallow bays, the fish found warmer water on long, shallow points that stretched as far as the center of the lake to near the original river channel.

For the most part, I used my MotorGuide bow-mount electric to keep the boat in about seven feet of water. I could cast jigs into two feet of water and bring them back as well as casting parallel to the structure and probing to the seven-foot depths. My best presentation was a 1/8 ounce jig with the biggest fathead minnow I could find. These active fish were in the shallow water feeding on the emerald shiners that had moved in to spawn. Again, find the food and you'll find the walleyes. That's how I won the tournament.

TROUBLE-SHOOTING TIP

Cover Territory For Post-Spawn Walleyes

When searching shallow water from zero to 10 feet, you'll find your electronics are generally useless. Locate these shallow fish by trolling crankbaits. The fastest and most effective way is to use your main engine and troll. Short line your crankbaits so that they hit the bottom now and then. Try to cover as much territory as possible with a fast troll.

Once you have located aggressive fish, you may choose other presentations that could be more effective, such as casting a crankbait, jigs or perhaps even using a bottom bouncer. Remember, the key is to cover ground with crankbaits until you find aggressive fish.

WHAT ABOUT FALL WALLEYES?

Weather is the number one factor for fall walleyes. If it's going to be windy, cloudy or chilly, go hunting rather than fishing. When the sun warms and brightens those October and November days and the wind lays flat, load the boat and head out after big walleyes. The bite is on!

Just the fact that you're on the water fishing is 75 percent of the battle with fall fishing. Catching walleyes in the fall is easy if you just follow these four basic rules for lakes and reservoirs.

TROUBLE-SHOOTING TIP

Take Notes On Patterns

Keep a journal on fall walleye fishing every year. Record the dates, locations, water temperatures and weather conditions. These patterns will hold year after year.

Rule #1

Always locate walleyes with your electronics before you fish. Check all the main and longest points and stay out of the shallow bays. On long points, check all sides by zig-zagging from deep to shallow water until you locate fish. Don't expect to find the mother lode of fish at this time of the year, one or two fish on your electronics will signal the time to start fishing.

Rule #2

Slow is the key for fall walleyes. Walleyes are as cold

> **TROUBLE-SHOOTING TIP**
>
> **What Your Electronics Are Telling You**
> Remember, you don't have to see a number of fish on your electronics for a school of walleyes to be present. Take into consideration that your transducer's cone angle is generally 20 degrees. This means if you're in 30 feet of water, you're looking at a seven to eight-foot diameter circle. For 20 degree transducers, divide the depth by four to determine the diameter of the circle you're seeing on the bottom. For a 16 degree transducer, divide by five.

as the water and their attitude toward feeding will also be cold. This negative mood of the fish requires longevity in your presentation. Try to keep your bait in front of the fish as long as possible and give him ample time to react to the bait, move up to it, and suck it in.

This deep water fall presentation means light line with light jigs. A good choice to use is a 1/4 ounce jig with a big minnow on four or six-pound test line. Use your bow mount electric to move slowly so you can keep bottom contact with a light jig. Try to keep your line as vertical and close to the boat as possible. Don't allow the line to go past a 45-degree angle from the boat. If it does, you'll lose contact with the bottom. Again, cover the structure very slowly and concentrate on keeping track of the bottom with the jig.

Rule #3

Big minnows and big baits are very important in the fall. The ideal bait is a four to six inch minnow (chubs preferred) on a 1/4 ounce jig. Vertically jig your bait on top of the fish, and give the fish ample time to react by longevity in your presentation.

TROUBLE-SHOOTING TIP

Set The Hook On Anything You Feel

When fall fishing, set the hook whenever you feel anything. What you may feel and think is a wet leaf, a piece of debris, or a weed, could very likely be a fish. Many times late fall walleye hits are so light they go undetected. Time and time again, what I thought was a snag on the bottom turned out to be a big walleye.

Rule #4

Always use light line and light jigs. Remember, fish are very cold and need time to react to your bait. He's not sucking in a tremendous amount of water and not flaring his gills with the same power he would when the water temperature is warm. Very light line and heavy concentration are required for fall fishing. These techniques are worth it, and the reward is stretching your fishing season another 30 to 60 days with probably the best chance to nail a trophy.

120 **WALLEYE TROUBLE-SHOOTING**

Daryl Christensen Photo

Daryl Christensen with a lunker taken over the weed tops with a crankbait.

HOW DO YOU FIND WALLEYES IN WEEDS?

Understanding why walleyes use weeds is the first step in finding them. Although walleyes and weeds seem to go together, don't be confused. Walleyes don't like weeds! They can *use* weeds for cover, shade or security, but these are only conveniences that come with weeds, not their *real* reason to be there.

The real connection between the walleye and the weed bed is much simpler: FOOD! Small minnows, young-of-the-year perch, as well as most other young-of-the-year fish depend on weeds to provide food and cover to help get them through that vulnerable first year. The walleye is simply in the weeds searching out this easy food source. The walleye is simply there to eat.

You'll find that some weed beds can hold walleyes at different periods during the year and that some will hold walleyes year-around. Whether walleyes use weeds

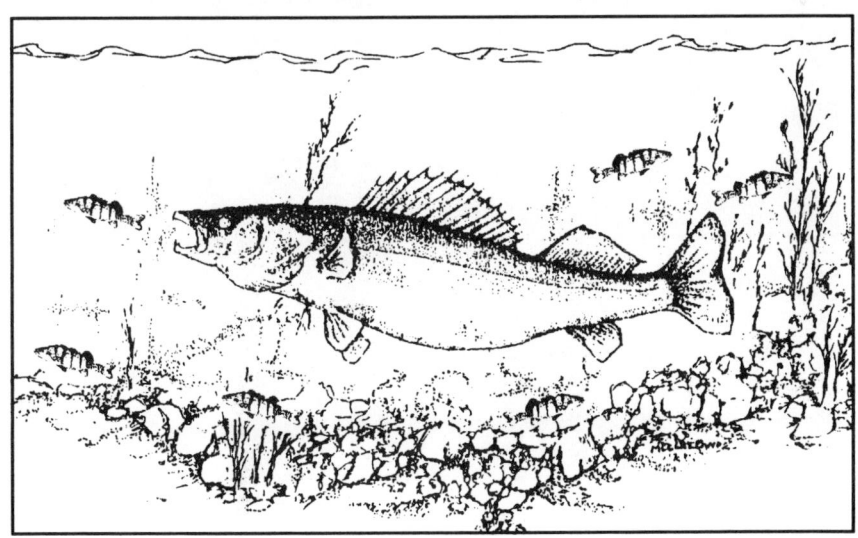

at all depends on the type of forage base (food) in the system. Specifically is there food in the weeds? Consider a reservoir that has a forage base that suspends - such as gizzard shad or smelt. It is unlikely that walleyes will be feeding in the weeds because suspended forage base fish are a much easier meal than chasing young-of-the-year perch through weeds. Always consider the forage base, and remember that walleyes will be after the easiest meal.

Don't try to identify the different types of weeds that walleyes may like better than others. Weeds are weeds! Some weeds hold baitfish and some don't. Understanding that there has to be food in the weeds for walleyes

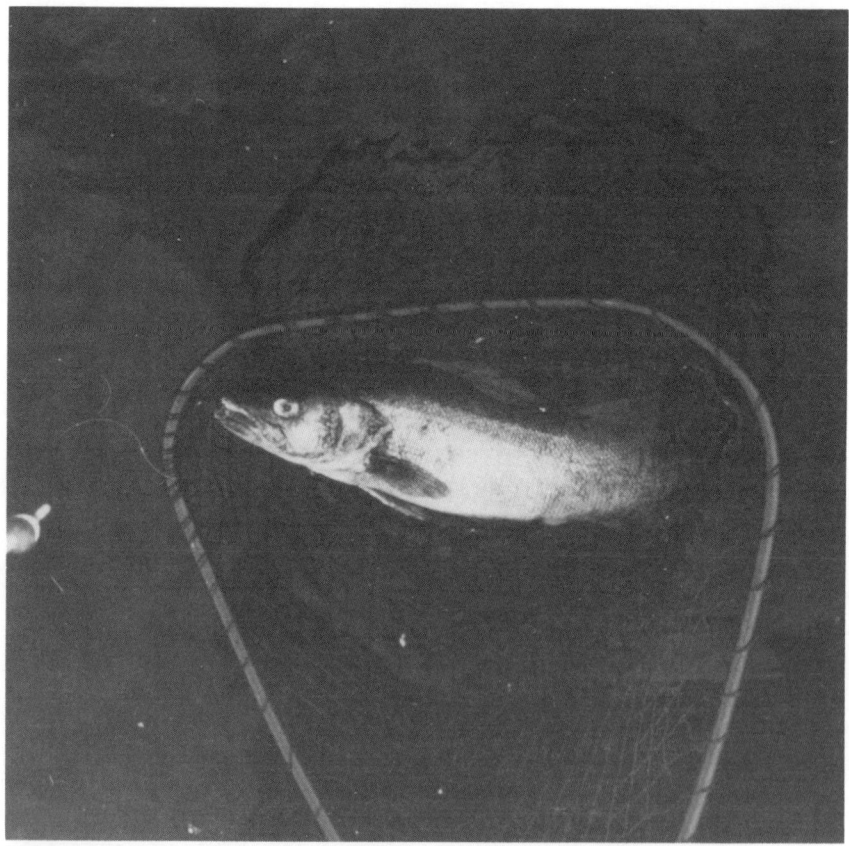

Slip bobbers, weeds, and walleyes go hand in hand.

to be present is the first step. The next step is to look for food in the weeds, not the walleyes. Visual aids are a big short cut in finding walleyes feeding in the weeds! Look for signs of life such as fish activity - minnows flipping on the surface, small fish surfacing for insects, or the weeds moving as a larger fish darts from his hiding place. These are all signs of life or activity, signs that the weeds are full of food and possibly walleyes.

Once a promising weedy area has been located, don't spend too much time fishing without success. Stick to the high-percentage spots such as the tip of the weed point or a saddle between two patches. Casting a crankbait along the weed edge is a quick way to cover a great deal of area. Once the fish are found, take your time and fine-tune your presentations in order to take as many fish as possible from that area. Be sure to take the time to note all of the physical attributes involved in and around the weeds. Concentrate on not necessarily what kinds of weeds or water depths are present, but on water temperature, time of day, water visibility and even the type of bottom. These things are the keys to reproducing the pattern that the baitfish are using and provide the key to locating weed walleyes in other parts of the lake.

TROUBLE-SHOOTING TIP

Take Advantage Of Night

When darkness falls and the wind lays down turning the water surface into glass, it's time to find weed walleyes.

With a bright spot-light in your boat, you can literally take an inventory on walleyes in the weeds. These fish can be recognized from as far as 50 feet away. Walleye eyes reflect light like a deer's eyes do when the animal is looking into a headlight. Not only will you find the key areas where walleyes are holding, but you'll also eliminate the weeds that aren't holding them.

Jim Kalkofen Photo

Jim Kalkofen, Executive Director of the PWT, is an expert on shallow walleyes on Lake Winnebago. He shows that BIG fish do live in shallow water!

HOW DO YOU FIND SHALLOW WATER WALLEYES?

I was a shallow water walleye enthusiast long before many anglers ever believed that fish could be taken regularly in one to two feet of water. It used to be that a walleye caught in shallow water was considered a fluke or an accident. I've found that almost everywhere I go, these "accidents" are waiting to happen. Shallow water walleyes are always worth looking for, whether you're fishing a tournament or out to catch a pan of fillets!

A wealth of information exists regarding shallow water walleyes and to cover it all here would be impossible. Still, the question "How do You find shallow water walleyes?" remains one of my more frequently asked questions at seminars all around the country.

Although shallow water walleyes can be found and fished all season long, spring is the most productive time to find them. Spring brings the spawn which brings the walleyes to shallow waters to lay their eggs. They are then warmed and aerated by the increased water movement in the shallows. These warm, shallow waters are also where the highest concentration of food will be found. Minnow and fry activity is increased where suspended particles cloud the water, and new weed growth is found. Walleyes will remain in these shallow waters as long as these microscopic food sources are abundant.

TROUBLE-SHOOTING TIP

Golden Rule

There's one golden rule to finding shallow water walleyes: "Fish the fish before you spook them."

Remember the "golden rule" for walleyes in shallow water: "Fish the fish before you scare them." The biggest problem you face with walleyes in shallow water is that you can't see them ahead of time, and they're easily spooked into deeper water. Just because you can't see them, doesn't mean they're not there. Now that we've addressed the fact that walleyes can be found in shallow water at any time during the year, let's look at some short cuts to finding them.

TROUBLE-SHOOTING TIP

Visual Aids

Visual aids are the key to finding walleyes in shallow water. Not only do visual aids tell you that walleyes could be in the area, but also, more importantly, visual aids help eliminate the majority of the shallow water.

Wind

Before looking for likely walleye hot spots, let's look where they're not. Elimination of unlikely waters is a great short-cut. If the wind is blowing, you can eliminate half the water, the half the wind is NOT blowing into! Shallow water walleye success depends on wind and wave action.

Mud-Lines

Wave action against a shoreline or an exposed point often washes small particles of dirt into the water creating what we refer to as "mud-lines." This "mud" suspends in the top two feet of water. It moves along the points or banks, eventually spreading over a large area. When a new mud-line starts to develop, it's like ringing the dinner bell. There's an immediate movement of fish into the shallow water. The fry begin to eat the suspended particles and to enjoy the safety of the dark water. Larger fish begin to dine on the fry, and you guessed it, the walleyes will soon arrive to feed.

Banks

Once you have narrowed down the search for hot spots on the windy side, you can now check out bank structure. Studying bank structure is another method to quickly eliminate unlikely walleye holding areas. Always eliminate gradually sloping banks such as beaches. Why? As the water on beaches gradually shallows, it allows the small baitfish to escape farther onto the bank than their larger predators. Instead, look for banks with bumpers or lips. This structure enables a walleye to corner its prey.

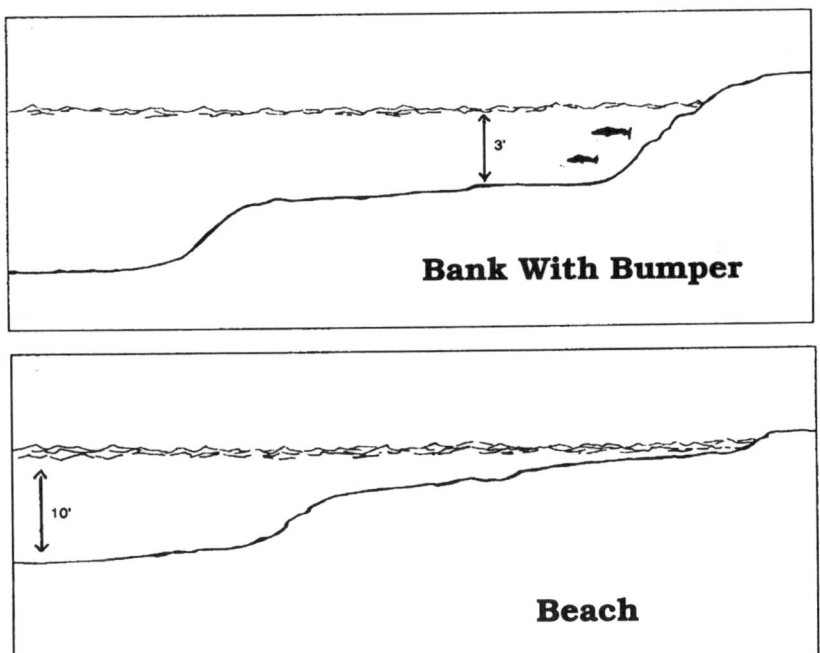

The upper example shows a bumper in deeper water tight against the shoreline, perfect for walleyes to trap bait fish. With a beach shoreline, bait fish have the advantage.

Dark Water

"Dark" water is a section of a lake (due to iron, inlets, bog stain, soft bottom) or stretches of shoreline with low visibility. If you look closely, you'll notice that even small lakes exhibit variations in water clarity. A certain bank for example, may be composed of gravel and another one of silt. Guess which one will be darker, even without a wind?

Night Lights

One trick I've pioneered for locating walleyes in shallow water is "shining" with a spotlight at night. I know that any fish I find in shallow water structure at night will often use the same areas during the day (provided fishing pressure hasn't driven them off). Many fish will use the same rock on a rock pile, and all you have to do is remember where it is! Not only will you locate the areas that are holding the most fish, but you'll quickly eliminate 90 percent of the shallow water that holds nothing.

Active Deep Fish

Other boats catching fish in nearby deep water are also a good clue. Anytime you see fish coming out of deep water on a long point, be aware that walleyes could be farther up the point as shallow as two feet.

Once you've located walleyes in shallow water, fine-tune your presentations. Try slip bobbers (especially in weeds), toss jigs into six inches of water, and on windy days try drifting with a bottom bouncer and spinner.

Boat Docks

There's one more visual aid for locating shallow-water walleyes, one that most anglers rarely consider: rod holders. When you survey the docks on a lake, and you see a certain section where the docks are rigged with landing nets and rod holders, it's a rather safe bet that there's a reason for it. Walleyes as well as other fish are using that particular shoreline. Believe it or not, this is one of the first things I look for on an unfamiliar lake.

Keep these tips in mind and remember, shallow water fishing is all done visually (no electronic fish finders). You'll need to choose methods of presentation that will allow you to remain away from the fish and cover maximum amounts of water. Long casts from the boat or trolling a shallow running crankbait with planer boards can greatly increase your odds.

TROUBLE-SHOOTING TIP

Walleyes In Shallow Water

Oh! By the way, I've already written an entire book on shallow water walleyes coincidentally called <u>Walleyes In Shallow Water</u>. This book reveals in detail more of my easy-to-understand theories, secrets, and techniques of shallow water walleyes that can be put into action on your next fishing trip. You can purchase <u>Walleyes In Shallow Water</u> from Fishing Enterprises, P.O. Box 7108, Pierre, SD 57501, or call 1-800-223-9126.

130 WALLEYE TROUBLE-SHOOTING

HOW DO YOU CATCH WALLEYES AFTER A COLD FRONT?

Let's address this age old question with simple logic. First, what is a cold front? It can be a 40-degree temperature drop, a vicious rumbling thunderstorm, or a howling north wind. A cold front could be all of the above or none of the above. Who cares? You're not going to fish until after it passes anyway!

Recognizing cold front conditions after the cold front has passed can be tricky and often can be hidden behind the disguise of a perfect fishing day. Yes, "the perfect fishing day." It's the day you've invited your boss or talked your buddy into taking the day off work. It's a day of weather so perfect that the words "cold front" never enter your mind, at least not until the day is over and you're trying to explain to your buddy why you didn't catch a single fish. Failure to recognize a cold front is the major reason for many days each year of poor fishing success.

Learn to expect, recognize and accept cold front conditions.

Expect A Cold Front

When you say to yourself, "This great fishing is too good to last," and everything you do works, look out! Here comes a cold front. As my old fishing partner Bob Propst, Sr., would always say, "If you have two good days of walleye fishing in a row, look out for the third!"

Recognizing A Cold Front

Consider the following scenario: The bite has been

tremendous for the last couple days, and you're hoping the wind will go down along with the temperature. As you pull into the boat landing the next morning, your wishes have been granted. As you look out over the water, you feel giddy with anticipation; the wind has stopped, the surface of the lake is "looking like glass." The sun is shining in a clear blue sky, and it's 20 degrees cooler then it was yesterday. It's going to be the perfect fishing day - WRONG! It's a "MAJOR COLD FRONT." Recognize it! Too often the most perfect fishing day of the year is often the worst fish-catching day of the year.

TROUBLE-SHOOTING TIP

Recognize A Cold Front And Change Your Game Plan Immediately!

Don't wait until the drive home to say to your buddies, "Boy, that cold front really shut down those walleyes. I wonder where they went?"

Accept Cold Front Conditions

As the weather changes, so should you! Don't continue using the same strategies that worked the day before. If you've made your first pass on yesterday's fish and didn't get a hit, don't change color, don't change bait, don't change presentations. Those tactics won't work. No matter what you do, you can't catch fish that aren't there! Accept the fact that this is a cold front and that the fish have moved. New locations and major presentation changes are in order. Cold fronts trigger a defensive reaction in walleyes. Walleyes, whose entire focus had been to seek food yesterday, will be seeking security today.

Regardless of the time of the year, think of cold front fishing as if it were fall fishing. The methods and locations are the same.

QUESTION 31 — HOW DO YOU CATCH WALLEYES AFTER A COLD FRONT?

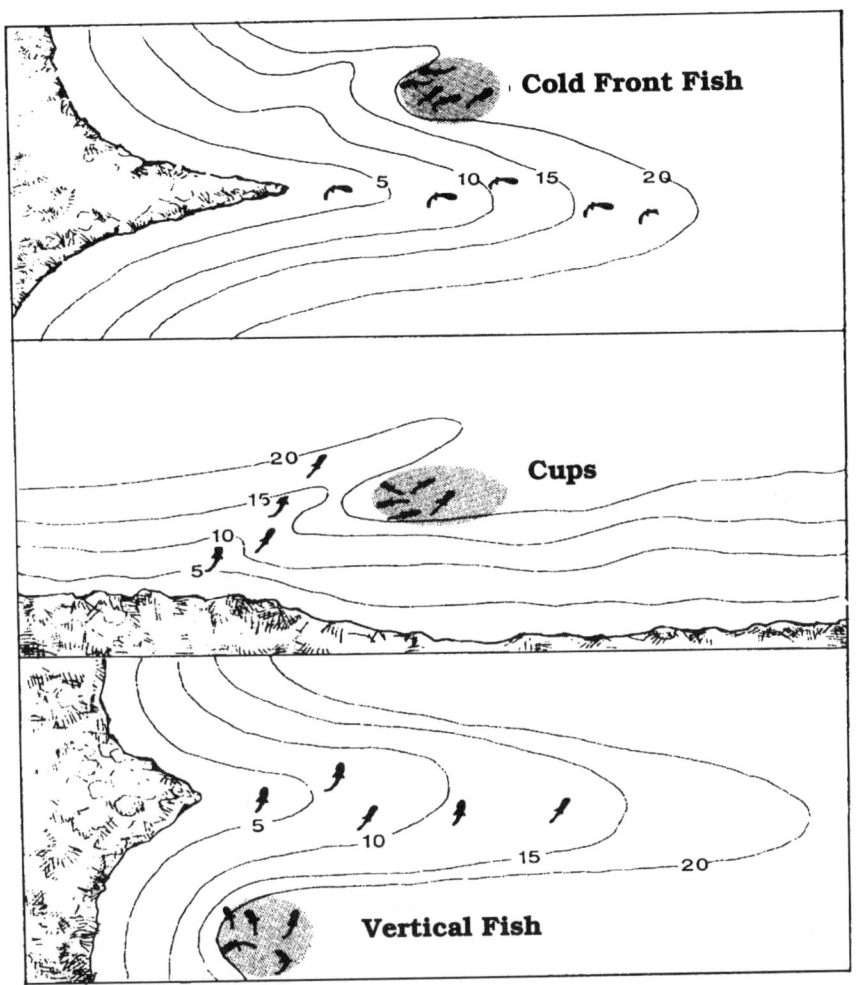

The fish located on the top of the breaks are typical hot summertime fish looking for a meal. The fish in the shaded areas are these same fish after a cold front has moved them to secure areas, such as cups and vertical drop-offs.

If you have had hot fish scattered on a flat or on the top of a long shallow point before the cold front comes through, they will be gone, but not far. Use your electronics and start checking the closest drop-offs, at depths of anywhere from 10 to 30 feet. Check the steepest drops on a break and be on the look-out for inside turns or corners (cups) on these structures. You'll find that with good electronics, cold front fish are easy to locate. You will also find that these fish are hard to catch.

Cold front fish are "cold fish." They'll be in deeper water and tightly schooled on the most vertical structure. Cold fish need time to react. Use a presentation with longevity, such as vertical jigging or dragging a Lindy Rig slowly through them. Patience is the key. Fish slowly and quietly with the confidence of knowing that they will eventually bite.

Bob Propst, Jr., with a nice cold front fish, knows patience is the key to success.

ARE THERE SUSPENDED WALLEYES IN MY LAKE?

Yes! Do you remember the time old so-and-so was trolling blindly across the middle of the lake and accidentally caught a 10-pound walleye? That wasn't an accident. The fish were there and always had been.

I fish suspended fish; it's still new to me, and I am by no means an expert on the subject. To be fair to you, I asked an expert on suspended fish, Gary Parsons. He has been catching suspended walleyes in lakes and reservoirs across North America for nearly 20 years. Here's his answer:

I think all bodies of water have suspended walleyes at certain times of the year. The real question should be whether or not they are catchable. It has been my experience that angling success is totally dependent on the number of walleyes versus how much food a system has to offer. For example, if a lake has a high population of walleyes and very little food, the walleyes will definitely roam the open water looking for food. These fish are highly catchable. Conversely, if the system has good numbers of fish but is also leaded with forage, there may still be large numbers of fish in the open water; however, they may be impossible to catch because it is impossible for your one crankbait to compete with Mother Nature! Every lake will have its own set of circumstances. Some will have very few fish and a great deal of bait. Some will have a few fish and very little food.

The only way to know if your water has a catchable group of walleyes is to go out and try your luck. Concentrate on lake flats from 10 to 50 feet deep. Look extensively with your electronics for the actual presence of fish. Note the depths in which they are located, and posi-

tion your crankbaits slightly above the main groups by trolling through them. Don't be afraid to position one of the baits in the top six feet of water. Many times that is exactly where open water feeding takes place. If the cranks don't work and the lake is known to have a good spinner bite, try trolling spinners. You may find the fishing experience of your dreams!

That's the answer I would have given - after a few more years of practice. Now that you've heard from the expert, do you really understand what he said? Do It and you will!

TROUBLE-SHOOTING TIP
Always Run A High Line

Walleyes can be suspended extremely shallow over deep water and you'll not be able to detect them with your electronics because you'll spook them with the boat. Plus, fish you read on your electronics can also be deeper than they normally are. Remember, you just ran over them with the boat! Always run a shallow bait a few feet from the surface on a trolling board to check for these fish.

Part IV

WHAT YOU NEED TO DO

Keep It Simple & Smile!

138 WALLEYE TROUBLE-SHOOTING

HOW CAN I GET A BETTER HOOK-SET?

We've all watched fishermen on TV set the hook with "gusto." Many opinions about the topic of "setting the hook" exist, especially with walleyes. It's important to examine the hook-setting techniques on a walleye simply and logically. Forget about the "Hollywood Hook-Set," portrayed by too many TV fishermen.

Listening to clever sayings such as, "Set it hard enough to rip his lips off," often give fishermen a false picture. Hooking walleyes is really quite simple. If it was as difficult as some fishermen would have us believe and required so much strength to drive the hook home, fishermen, especially kids, wouldn't have much luck in catching walleyes.

When you consider that kids and walleyes go together, youngsters do a good job when it comes to hooking and landing fish. Why? Quite simply! With walleyes you don't have to tip the boat over when setting the hook. (That technique may look good on television, but it has absolutely nothing to do with hooking walleyes.)

In order to better understand what setting the hook is all about, find a friend, take your fishing rod outside, and peel off about 50 feet of line, and tie on your favorite crankbait. The next step is to grab the back of the lure in your hand and hold it tight while your buddy attempts to set the hook hard. Keep a firm grip on the lure, and you'll discover you barely feel a tug on the line when he tries to set the hook. After you've completed this experiment, you'll realize that as long as you have a firm grip on the lure, hooks could never be driven into your hand, let alone into the mouth of a toothy walleye.

The lesson from the experiment is easy to compre-

Mike holds the hook-set until the fish opens his mouth.

hend: as long as the walleye - or you - have hold of the bait, the holder can't be hooked. With a firm grasp on the bait combined with line stretch and steady pressure from the rod tip, the lure will never start to penetrate the walleye or your hand. Warning: DON'T LET GO, or you'll be hooked for sure. That's how you hook walleyes; have pressure on the bait when the fish opens his mouth to get rid of it.

You can always tell if an angler is fishing for walleyes because he'll be seen reaching high in the sky with his rod when he sets the hook. He'll also be standing on his tip toes with both arms overhead, trying to keep pressure on the walleye until the fish opens his mouth. It is as simple as that. Once a walleye opens his mouth and removes the pressure (and his teeth), the bait will move or slip and a hook can now penetrate.

TROUBLE-SHOOTING TIP

Sharp Hooks

It is very hard to drive a hook through the mouth of a walleye. If you have ever re-hooked a walleye for a photo, you know how tough his mouth is. Try to re-hook a walleye this summer with a sharp hook then use a dull hook. This will make you a firm believer that it is mandatory to use sharp hooks at all times.

You have to realize that walleyes have a very hard mouth with numerous teeth. Examine a crankbait on which you've caught a walleye. Have you noticed they're often punched full of holes. As long as a walleye has the pressure of his teeth squeezing into your bait, you can't set the hook. The key is to hold the hook-set until the fish opens his mouth and allows the bait and hooks to slip. How do you know when a walleye opens his mouth? When you feel the rod jerking in a pumping motion, the fish has opened his mouth. His gills have flared, and he's thrashing side to side. You can almost tell how big the walleye is by the length of the stroke from side to side. Short jerks indicate a short fish; the longer the stroke, the bigger the fish. Remember, keep maximum pressure on the walleyes during this stage; it is now that the hooks are working their way into the hard part of the walleye's mouth.

Another important factor to consider is hook size. Use large, sharp hooks for greater success. Small hooks in hard mouths with many teeth don't mix. I use a #1 or #2 Aberdeen hook with live bait. This light wire hook has a wide gap for maximum hooking. On crankbaits, I use only Excalibur rotating treble hooks.

Keep the hook-setting tips in mind on your next outing, and you'll have more walleyes in your freezer.

South Dakota Tourism Photo

HOW DO YOU PREVENT SHORT-HITS?

To prevent a short-hit, you must first recognize what a short-hit is. A short-hit can be one of many things ranging from the fish biting off half a nightcrawler to taking the whole minnow to a crankbait tap. It can amount to just a single ring around a bobber. "Short-hits" basically mean a fish attempted to eat the bait but was somehow prevented. The solution for short-hits is to allow the fish to eat. Any time you experience a short-hit, it means only one thing, a fish did the best job it could to take the bait, but your presentation didn't allow for success. It's your fault, but you can fix it. Lighter line and lighter bait is the first step in eliminating short-hits.

Let's use jigging as an example, which is a presentation that is notorious for short-hits. Here are some quick and easy cures. Start with this question, "Why do 90 percent of the hits while jigging come as the jig is falling?" The popular belief is that a fish eases up to the jig and will wait for it to fall before he hits. WRONG! A walleye doesn't care if the jig is falling or rising. A walleye will hit the jig as many times on the way up as he does on the way down. Walleyes make reactions, not decisions.

What happens is simple. As an angler lifts his rod, the jig comes off the bottom and zips through the water. At the same time, a walleye will try to suck in the jig and the surrounding water into its mouth. The jigging stroke merely pulls the bait and jig out of the flow of water going into the walleye's mouth. Most of the time, anglers don't even know that a hit has just happened, even though it was a sincere effort on the walleye's part.

Stroking a jig up pulls it out of the fish's mouth and prevents success. If an angler is letting his jig fall when the walleye sucks in the bait, the jig is allowed to flow freely with the water into the walleye's mouth with very little line resistance. As a jig falls, you've simply created slack line that allows the jig to go with the flow of water and bingo, fish on!

If you understand how a walleye feeds and concentrate on what you can do to allow this to happen, you're success is going to increase. Use your imagination and create presentations that will allow a walleye to eat. Remember, the jig and bait will always travel with the flow of water into the walleye's mouth. When this happens, it pulls a certain amount of line through the water. This is the resistance that creates short-hits, and this is the reason for light line. If you cut the line diameter in half, you can cut resistance in half.

Consider stinger hooks as another option. Although they're not my first choice, they can be very effective in

---

TROUBLE-SHOOTING TIP

Short-hits; Lighten-up

A walleye inhales a bait rather than biting it. Stop those short-hits by using lighter line. Thick, bulky line has more resistance when pulled through the water and might cause a walleye to miss or short-hit. Light line is the answer. It allows the bait to flow easily into the fish's mouth as he inhales the water surrounding it.

Light line or a smaller line diameter plays a huge part in allowing a walleye to inhale a bait with the flow of water. If the bait wasn't attached to a fishing line, a walleye would have little trouble sucking the bait into his mouth. But, because we do have line attached, there is more resistance creating difficulty for walleyes to suck in the bait.

The rule is simple - if you're having short-hits, lighten up.

eliminating short-hits. When all else fails, including the lightest jig with the lightest line, a stinger hook can save the day.

Let's take a quick look at bottom bouncers and spinners. The cure here for short-hits is easy. Fish them with the right attitude, concentrating on keeping track of the bottom. Do this by only letting out enough line so that the bottom bouncer is just off the bottom. Then, by dropping the rod tip, allow the bottom bouncer to just barely touch bottom. By continually repeating this motion, you will keep track of the bottom, and every time the bouncer touches bottom, it will stop. The spinner will continue its forward motion, overriding and creating the slack needed for the walleye to inhale the bait.

If you're using a straight leader and a hook with a bottom bouncer, attach a styrofoam float to the center of the leader. This is a cure for short-hits with your bottom bouncer and can also be applied to your Lindy or Roach Rig leaders. This set-up also allows fish to inhale the bait on the first try, thus eliminating the need to release line. It allows you to set the hook the moment a hit is felt.

Short-Hits On Crankbaits

To recognize a short-hit on a crankbait, you need to understand "cranking" as an art. For example, when trolling crankbaits, have you ever noticed that when you make a turn, the inside rod usually catches the fish? This happens because the slack line allows the fish to eat. If you have the opportunity, use trolling patterns which resemble "S" curves which increase the speed on the outside rod, and decrease the speed on those inside. This action not only slows the crankbait down, but also creates a bow of slack line which makes it easier for a fish to inhale the bait.

When trolling, you can feel the crankbaits vibration as you grip the rod. On occasions you may think you

146 WALLEYE TROUBLE-SHOOTING

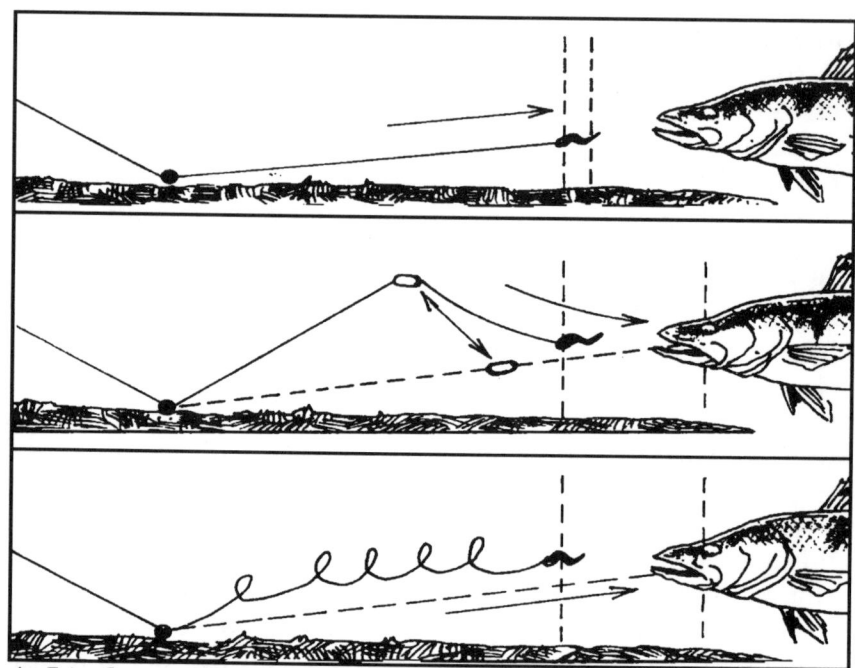

A Lindy or Roach Rig (top) doesn't have enough slack between the bait and the weight, as floats (center) or coiled leaders (bottom) do.

feel something and instinctively pull the rod forward to clear it from any weeds or trash it may have picked up. Then as you drop the rod back - BOOM! the fish hits. What you felt at first was the initial short-hit the fish made. The fish was right behind the bait, perhaps touching it or just sucking enough water around the lure to disturb its synchronized wobble. By jerking the rod ahead, the lure also moved ahead. As you dropped the rod back, you created slack which allowed the fish to take the lure. A good rule to follow is: "Anytime you feel anything, drop the rod back."

The technique of dropping the rod back also applies when using weight-forward spinners. When you feel something as you reel in the spinner, drop the rod back; if your blade stops spinning or has lost tension, drop the rod back. Chances are a fish is behind the spinner and has sucked in enough water past the bait to actually

QUESTION 34   HOW DO YOU PREVENT SHORT-HITS?   147

force the blade against the shaft of the spinner. Drop the rod tip, create the slack, and allow the fish to eat!

The cure for short-hits when casting crankbaits is to work the crankbait with a "stop and go" retrieve. Choose a bait that is as close as possible to being "neutral buoyant," such as a Rouge. After casting, crank the bait down to the desired depth and retrieve it in three-foot strokes of the rod by pulling the rod tip up. Take up slack all the way to the boat. Try dropping the rod tip and stopping the bait on a break where shallow water turns to deep, or stopping the bait at the edge of a weed line.

Bobbers are subject to short-hits as well. The same philosophy applies, whether it's slip bobbers or straight bobbers for panfish. When you see a ring around the bobber, this tells you the same thing that the rod does when you feel a little "tap." The line has just stopped the bait from flowing into the fish's mouth.

Three rings in succession means the fish has unsuccessfully tried to get the bait into his mouth three times. Because not enough slack line exists between the

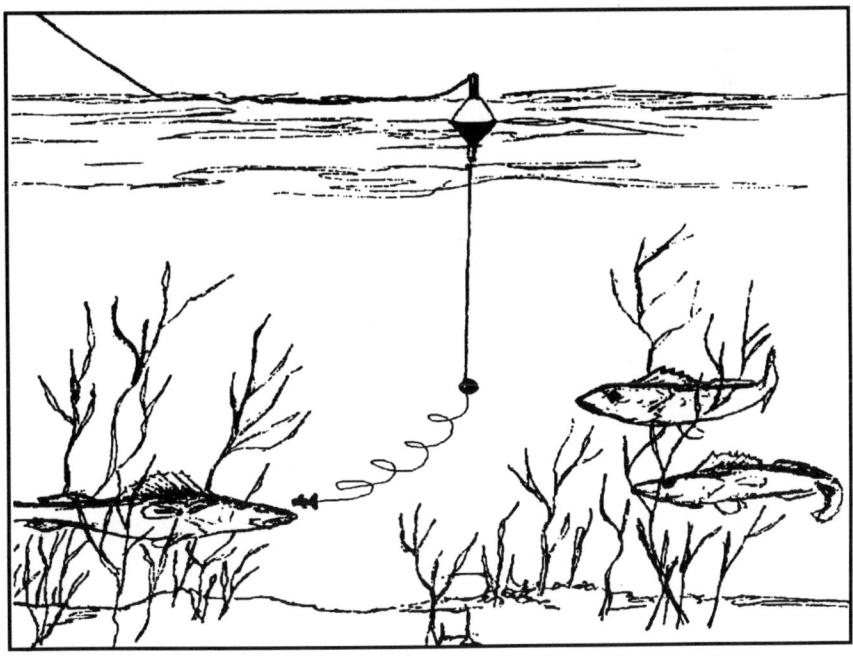

bobber and the bait, the bobber stops the bait from going into the fish's mouth. The presentation with a bobber is successful when it disappears without any resistance.

For bobber fishing, I like a coiled leader of four to six-pound test line for the necessary slack (take it off an old spool that has remained coiled). Use a two-foot piece from the split-shot to the hook. This gentle coil will draw the baited hook towards the weight and still give plenty of slack for the fish to take the bait when straightening out the coils. Without any resistance, the fish takes the bait, the bobber disappears, and the fish swims off with the bait in its mouth.

If you understand how a fish eats, eliminating short-hits is easy and rewarding. Just use your imagination and the right attitude; you'll increase your catch tremendously.

WHAT'S YOUR FAVORITE ALL-AROUND TECHNIQUE?

If you had to choose one method out of all the different techniques we use in walleye fishing, what would it be? Would you choose crankbaiting, jigging a spoon, slip bobbers, bottom bouncers...? There's no question, the hands-down winner has to be the versatile jig.

The jig, simply because of its success in so many different situations, has applications for use at any depth, and its ease to change characteristics in size and color to make it the winner. For example, consider its versatility. The jig is so unlike many other presentations because of the following:

• You can fish jigs in two to 50 feet of water.

• You can make a jig tiny or big.

• Changing colors, weight, size and live bait is done easily and quickly;

• Jigs are available in most stores and are cheap.

• No other method gives total control of presenting a bait to the fish; it's literally a direct line between the fishermen and the fish.

• You can give a jig a certain type of action, and if it doesn't work, the action can be changed again and again until the fish react.

• When you find finicky fish, it's one of the best presentations an angler can use.

• All sizes and species of fish are susceptible to a jig!

The most attractive features of jig fishing though is its ease to use. Often considered as difficult, demanding fine-tuned expensive rods and years of practice, jig fishing is actually very easy. Anyone can do it. With the right attitude, jig fishing is the simplest for presentation and one of the best producers I know.

The proper attitude for jig fishing success is also simple; it consists of two rules:

1) Use your jig simply to keep track of the bottom whether drifting, trolling, casting or vertical jigging. As you fish, simply lift the jig off the bottom and drop it back down until it touches. Repeat this and remember how the bottom feels and keep track of it.

2) Forget about trying to *make* fish bite! Forget about trying to *feel* a hit! Simply keep track of the bottom and set the hook if you feel anything at all. Set the hook if you think you're snagged; set the hook if you feel a tick, set the hook if you think you feel *anything*. Remember, it costs nothing to set the hook, and you'll be amazed how often those suspicions of what could have been a fish, turn into a fish!

With a little practice, jigs can open up a whole new world of fishing for you. You'll learn to read depths by the length of time it takes your jig to settle to the bottom. You'll be able to feel a hump or the slightest drop off and map the shape of an underwater structure to mentally paint an underwater picture. A complete picture with drop-offs, angles, weeds, and rocks that are where the fish are holding will be yours.

HOW DO YOU KNOW WHEN TO SWITCH PRESENTATIONS?

The appropriate time to switch presentations poses a problem that deserves a definite answer. Do I change when the wind changes, when the sun comes out, when the sun goes down? If you're looking for direct answers to these questions, you're going to be disappointed as there are no absolutes. Whether it's early in the day, high-noon, or about quitting time, the one rule never changes - FISH LOCATION DICTATES PRESENTATION!

Once you've located fish, the first thing to do is consider the presentation to use. Choose one that puts the odds in your favor by presenting a bait where the most fish are for the longest time. Now concentrate on fine-tuning that presentation by changing colors, sizes, speeds and/or even baits in order to keep the best presentation that puts the odds in your favor. If there is an appropriate time to switch presentations, it would sim-

---

TROUBLE-SHOOTING TIP

Fishing Or Going Fishing?

To make the most out of your fishing day, you must know the difference between when you're "fishing," and when you're "going fishing." Understand that the only time you're "fishing" is when you have a bait presented in a manner that allows the fish (if they are present) to eat. Should you choose to cast, whether it be a jig, a crankbait or a weight forward spinner, you'll automatically forfeit half your fishing day. You have to realize that all the time the bait is in your hand or sailing through the air and sinking slowly to the fish zone, you're not fishing, you're "going fishing."

ply be when you have changed locations. The only other time to switch presentation is when others around you are catching fish and you're not!

Automatic presentation changer.

WHY HAVE CRANKBAITS BECOME SO POPULAR?

Several reasons exist for the soaring popularity of crankbaits; the main reason is SUCCESS. I can safely say, "Crankbaits catch bigger fish." Why? I can't answer that question for sure. There are many theories ranging from "crankbaits attract the more aggressive fish," assuming aggressive fish are

Angling Communications Photo

bigger, to "crankbaits can be presented to fish that don't follow the traditional walleye habits," thus those fish are older and larger. Whatever the reason, I've seen crankbaits over the years take larger fish time and time again. Adding the baits' success to the simplicity of use, it's easy to see why the popularity of crankbaits has sky-rocketed in past years.

Because of their basic uses in trolling and casting, crankbaits can be over-simplified. Make no mistake, the degree of crankbaits' success depends on *your* knowledge of them.

The foundation of effective crankbait fishing is very simple; know the depth your crankbaits run. Until this knowledge is in hand, all the other crankbait questions are very insignificant. After all, if you can't get the bait to the fish, how could color, shape, action, or models of crankbaits make any difference whatsoever?

To answer the depth question, I contracted with ten of the leading crankbait manufacturers to test and document the exact trolling and casting depths of 200 of the most popular crankbaits. When the initial testing was completed, I went a step further and tested the depth of each bait on five different line sizes at 10-foot increments of line length. This crankbait depth information is now available in my "Crankbait Depth Guide & Calculator."

In the process of testing, which took 18 months, I learned much more about crankbaits than just the depths they may run. Here are some of the hard facts learned about hard baits:

Crankbait Classification

While testing 200 crankbaits, I discovered that crankbaits fit neatly into two broad categories of lures which perform similarly within their groups.

Rollers - These lures have the line-attaching eye in the nose, not the lip. They generally run shallow, requiring greater speeds to achieve their proper tight, side-to-side roll action.

Wobblers - These lures have the line-attaching eye in the lip. They will run deeper than rollers and require less speed to achieve their proper action. These lures zig-zag through the water on a wider plane than "rollers." The width of the side-to-side movement does not necessarily have a relationship to depth; however, this action helps the lures maintain maximum depths when line diameter is increased. The width of the lure's side-to-side travel is created by placing the line-attaching eye in the lip. Depth is dictated by the surface area of the lip; the larger the lip, the deeper a lure will run.

What Causes Lures to Dive?

The major factor that causes lures to dive is the surface area of the lip. The larger the surface area, the deeper the lure will run, providing the line-attaching eye is in the lip rather than the nose of the lure. Angles and shapes of the lips are not critical; size is the determining factor.

The Variable of Line Diameter

Line diameter regulates the depths lures will run when trolling or casting. The depth relationship is constant and a tool for controlling depth. For every line size decrease (such as #10 to #8), your crankbait will run about one foot deeper. The opposite is also true. For every line size increase, the lure runs about one foot less. The very shallow running lures and the deepest running lures may vary slightly from the "one foot" rule per line size.

Use line size to control depth. For example, if your favorite lure runs at 17 feet on #8 line and you want to use it at 15 feet, change to #12 line. Remember, as you go to heavier line, casting distance decreases.

Line Size for Trolling

Of the 40 fish that hit the crankbaits being tested, only six fish were caught. They were all caught while running 17-pound test line. We actually had more hits on eight and 12-pound test line but couldn't hook them because of the line stretch. These 40 strikes occurred directly below our research boat and were captured on our graph paper. Several times fish would grab the lure and take it completely out of the cone angle of our chart recorder. Most of these hits (on #8 and #12 line) went unnoticed by the researcher holding the rod; however, all strikes on #17 line were detected. Because of the tremendous stretch in light monofilament line, I recommend heavier line and extremely sharp hooks when trolling.

The Importance of Speed

Trolling speed does not influence lure depth within the lure's performance range. A crankbait pulled from one to four mph will not vary in depth. At less than one mph, most lures begin to rise. Over four mph, they also rise because of line resistance (drag). The exceptions are the speed-controlled lures like the Rat-L-Spot, due to gravity. The slower you pull these lures, the deeper they run. For this reason, we tested these lures at a fixed speed of 2.5 mph. Each lure has a best performance/speed range. Generally, deep diving lures should be run slower more than shallow running lures. Select those lures that operate best at similar speeds when trolling. During the casting research, all lures ran shallower with a faster retrieve.

When casting crankbaits, the average comfortable cranking speed for a bait casting reel is 100 cranks per minute. Although 100 cranks per minute is an average cranking speed, actual lure speed is dictated by the reel's gear ratio. The style of a lure dictates the most effective gear ratio.

QUESTION 37   **WHY HAVE CRANKBAITS**   157
                  BECOME SO POPULAR?

Jim Kalkofen Photo

Crankbaits: simple, easy to use, and effective.

To help anglers choose the proper reel for the style of baits they prefer, we converted retrieve ratios to miles per hour. At the average 100 cranks per minute on the 3.8:1 reel, retrieval speed is about 1.6 mph. The best lures for this speed are the deeper diving crankbaits. With the 5.2:1 medium fast retrieve reel, retrieval speed is 2.1 to 2.2 mph. This is the all-around choice. By cranking slower or faster, an angler can cover the widest variety of speeds. The fast 6.1:1 reel speed is 2.76 to 2.7 mph. This reel will easily move a bait at eight to 10 mph at maximum cranking speed.

Trolling Pattern Tips

If you're trolling a tight, oval-shaped or circular pattern in order to stay on a school of fish or a tiny piece of structure, lure choice is once again very important. On the inside rods, select lures that operate best at slower speeds, while outside rods should be set up with "faster" lures. This will produce the proper action on both sides of the boat throughout turns.

Tune Every Lure

To tune a crankbait to run straight, bend the line-attaching eye in the opposite direction that it's running. Always start with slight adjustments and keep testing. Use a needle nose pliers.

A) For lures with the eyelet in the lip, bend the eyelet slightly and evenly toward the side of the lip. Cast, retrieve, and test until perfect.

B) For lures with a metal lip and connecting link, use your fingers and bend the link in the middle. Don't bend the lip!

C) For lures with the eyelet in the nose, grasp the eyelet with a pliers and very carefully bend eyelet. Small adjustments are a must.

How Far Back?

The amount of line out has a great influence on a lure's depth. A shallow running lure will achieve its maximum depth on a shorter line. A deeper running lure requires more line.

After testing 200 lures, we determined that a 100 feet of line will let a lure achieve 80 percent of its maximum depth. At 120 feet, lures will run at or close to their maximum depth. With any slight gain in depth with additional line out, though you give up fish-hooking ability because of line stretch. If a greater distance from the boat is required because of clear water, use planer boards or side-liners to get the lures away from the boat's path rather than more line. It's important to know the length of line for successful trolling so fish-catching patterns can be repeated. There are several ways to accomplish this: count passes on a level wind reel, use a slip-bobber knot on the line, or put a line counter on the rod.

The Rod Angle Myth Exploded

The position of the rod tip, or rod angle, has the least affect on lure depth. When 100 feet or more of line is out while trolling, the rod tip can be 12 feet above the water or six feet underwater and the lure maintains its same depth. We tested a variety of shallow to deep-running lures to settle this theory for casting. On casts from 75 to 100 feet with each lure retrieved at the same speed, we held the rod as high overhead as possible. Then, we cast the same distance and retrieved the lure with the rod tip touching the water. The procedure was repeated with the rod completely submerged to the reel. The results were the same in all cases. The lure ran at exactly the same depth! If a lure is cast only a short distance and cranked instantly upon splash down with the rod tip held high, depth can be controlled by retrieval speed. If the line between the angler and the lure lays on the water, the angler loses control of depth; the lure will seek its natural depth, regardless of rod angles.

Never Troll Under the Fish

Trolling below suspended fish doesn't produce. Of the 40 fish that struck lures being tested and charted, all came from below the lure. Some traveled up as far as 30 feet to hit. Only the fish observed on the graph below the lure's track struck while those graphed above the lure did not react!

Rattles Are For Big Boys, Too

One of the biggest surprises from our testing dealt with rattles. More and more crankbait manufactures are molding BB's in air chambers within their lures. Thirty-five of the forty fish that hit the lures being tested along with the six that were caught, grabbed lures with rattles. All were captured on graph paper while the lures were running directly below our research boat. These lures accounted for all action and ran from eight to 32 feet deep. The only thing constant in 88 percent of the cases was that the lures were equipped with built-in rattles.

WHAT'S THE MOST IMPORTANT PART OF TROLLING?

The fact you ask this question means that you're already past the average angler on trolling knowledge. To the beginner, trolling seems simple. To those who "fish" a trolling system, rather than a simple troll, there are enough "wheres, whens, whys and whats" to fill the pages of this book.

I asked Rick LaCourse, my friend and top PWT tournament pro, to share what he believes are the three key considerations in fishing a trolling system. Believe me, with hundreds of days of trolling, not only in tournaments but also running one of the largest walleye guide services on Lake Erie, Rick not only fishes a trolling system, he may have invented it!

To many anglers, trolling is just an act of putting out your favorite crankbait and pulling it around until you catch something. At times this may work, but this hit-or-miss method of fishing is far from effective. To be efficient, there are several important elements you need to consider.

TROUBLE-SHOOTING TIP

Always Run A Bait Shallow

Always run a high line. Knowing the depth of shallow fish is almost impossible. You depend on your electronics, but there's nothing to see shallow. Realize the area you're looking at is the area you just ran over with your boat. What fish *were* shallow moved long before the back of your boat (where the transducer is located) passed over the area. Don't expect to see shallow fish on your electronics; assume they are there and always run a high line.

Professional tournament pro, Rick LaCourse with a Lake Erie crankbait victim.

QUESTION 38 — WHAT'S THE MOST IMPORTANT PART OF TROLLING?

With the aid of your electronics, attempt to find the location of the fish in relation to the structure of the lake you're fishing. Find out if the fish are holding tight to the points, inside cups, scattered along flats, holding on offshore humps or suspended over open water. Remember, if you don't see fish on your electronics, there's a chance they may be in very shallow. Depth is the key to successful trolling!

Depth

Trolling should actually be called 'controlled depth fishing.' Knowing where the bait is at all times is the key to a successful trolling pattern. After finding the fish, you need to match your presentation with the depth of the fish. To be able to do this, several decisions have to be taken into consideration. What bait are you going to use? What line diameter is best? How far back are your lures? Each of these elements affect the diving depth of the lure. To learn where your baits are running, you can experiment with all the variables or purchase Mike's 'Crankbait Depth Chart.' Use this chart to take the guesswork out of where your baits are running.

When more depth is needed than you have with the bait alone, you may elect to use a snap weight ahead of the lure to give added depth, or the use of wire line or weighted lead core line to get the lure down to where the fish are.

TROUBLE-SHOOTING TIP

Never Troll Under The Fish

Trolling below suspended fish doesn't produce. Of 40 fish that struck lures while they were being tested and charted for my "Crankbait Depth Guide," all came from below the lure. Some moved up as far as 30 feet to hit. Only the fish observed on the graph below the lure's track struck. Those graphed above the lure didn't react.

Lure Action

Next, you need to take into consideration the action of the lure needed to trigger a strike. Some of the elements to look at are the time of year, water temperature and daily weather conditions. Fish react differently to crankbaits during different times of the year. You need to know the varying actions of the lures along with the proper speeds needed to generate the appropriate action from them. During cold weather times when the water temperature is below 50 degrees, consider using a minnow-imitating bait like a Rattlin Rouge or Ripplin Redfin. These lures have a very enticing action when run at slow speeds.

As the water warms, begin running crankbaits that have a more aggressive action to them. These baits should be able to run faster speeds, around 1.7 mph and above, plus they should have a good, wide action to them. Running at higher speeds will allow you to present the bait to more fish and trigger them into striking. Lures to consider would be the Wally Diver, Wally Bomber and Bombers 24-A and 25-A. By paying close attention to the basics, your trolling patterns will be more productive.

TROUBLE-SHOOTING TIP

The Importance Of Speed

Trolling speed doesn't influence lure depth within the lure's performance range. A crankbait pulled from one to four mph has little variance in depth. At less than one mph, most lures begin to float. Over four mph, they rise because of line resistance (drag).

Generally, deep-diving lures should be run slower than shallow lures. Select lures that operate best at similar speeds when trolling.

Color Pattern

The last decision is the color pattern. Because a certain color worked the last time you fished does not mean it's going to work at another time under different conditions. To fish, color on crankbaits appears as 'flash patterns.' As the crankbait moves and rolls from side to side, the colors on the lure flash show in a strobe-like appearance, the brighter the finish the brighter the flash. Rainbow-colored finishes give a prism like flash as the colors mix and the lure rolls through the water. Consider using bright, metallic finished baits in water that's slightly stained to dirty for maximum flash. The more natural shad tones give a very soft flash and should be used in clear water conditions. Remember that at times small can be better as too much flash can scare away the fish.

LaCourse has covered several key parts that need to be addressed. Although they may even be the most important keys to successful trolling, they are only part of a complete trolling system.

The order in which you attach all the initial parts of trolling is of little importance. What is important is pattern reproduction. This is the ability to reproduce all the separate parts that made that particular system work - depth, speed, color, distance, current direction and wind. Eliminate what doesn't work; reproduce what does. That's trolling in a nut shell.

Mark Romanack Photo

Bruce DeShano, inventor and manufacturer of Off Shore Planer Boards, helps us all increase our trolling success.

WHEN & HOW SHOULD I TROLL?

How to troll is important, but understanding when to troll will help you put more fish in the boat.

Fish don't conveniently "hang out" where trolling is the best way to catch them. For instance, it's difficult to troll in flooded timber because you'll lose too many lures

and run out of "allowance money" in a hurry. Sharp structures with twists, turns, cups, and bends, do concentrate fish; however, trolled lures will pass in and out of these fish zones very quickly.

The most important aspect of trolling is depth. Hopeful, that message has been drilled home by now; when you plop a lure behind the boat, it'll fish at only one depth. Recognizing with electronics the depth of the fish, you will be guided by all the other "how-to" factors.

When fish are scattered over a large area at approximately the same depth, trolling should be the game plan. Generally, when fish are scattered and susceptible to trolling over a large flat or are suspended, they're hot and aggressive, out for lunch and actively feeding.

Under the How-to-Troll heading comes common sense. When dealing with scattered fish, the key is to present your lures to as many fish as possible. Spread your lures wide. Instead of three or four rods over the transom, covering an area 10 to 20 feet wide as you troll, put an eight or nine-foot rod out each side of the boat; and you'll easily cover over 25 feet of water. When you offer a smorgasbord of lures to three times as many fish, you've increased the odds in your favor. A step beyond the system is to spread lines even wider with Off

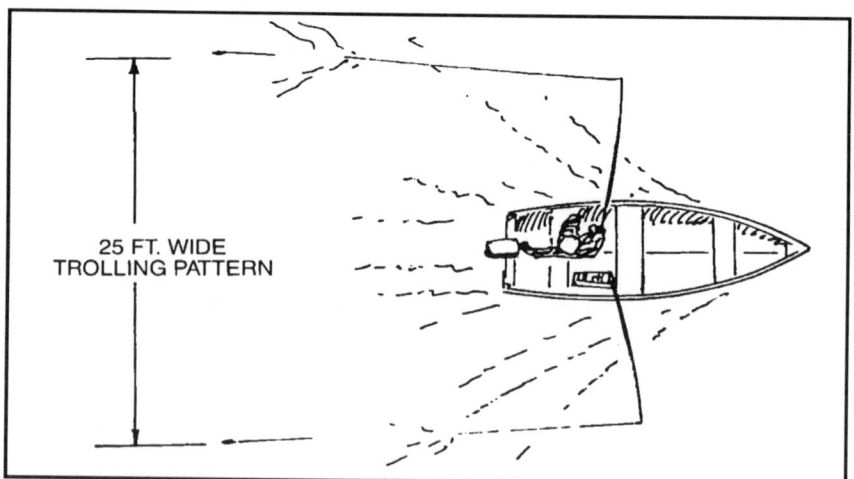

Outrigging helps cover territory.

Shore side planers or skis. These effective methods are explained in detail later.

Also, in the how-to department, I've mentioned covering water by staggering your lures horizontally if you have scattered fish at one depth. If they're showing up at various depths, spread your lures at different depths. If the fish are at 12 feet, use lures that run at 12 feet. If they're at 17, use the lure-line combination to reach 17 feet.

Match your lures to the fish zones, and when you catch two fish at the same depth, change half your lures to that depth. If you catch another, run all lures at that depth. If the action slows, then start experimenting by running lures at other depths where you're seeing individual fish on your electronics. You may also find other areas with similar structure to the initial area that really produced. When one spot slows down, find new water, but remember to check out the "hot spot" again. It will probably turn-on sometime again that same day.

Don't hesitate to beat your lures against the bottom if the bottom is relatively snag-free (we call it "clean"), and composed of sand, muck, fine gravel or small stones. Select a lure that runs deeper than the bottom. As the bait crashes into the bottom, it provokes fish or maybe wakes them up; they notice and react to an escaping intruder. Actually, when you consider life in the fish world, most movement is in short bursts either to eat or to escape being eaten. Perhaps the real explana

TROUBLE-SHOOTING TIP

Never Troll Under The Fish

Trolling below suspended fish doesn't produce. Of 40 fish that struck lures while they were being tested and charted for my "Crankbait Depth Guide & Calculator," all came from below the lure. Some traveled as far as 30 feet to hit. Only the fish observed on the graph below the lure's track struck; those graphed above the lure did not react.

tion why this bottom-crashing tactic catches fish is that it's easier for the fish to inhale the bait. Each time the lure hits bottom, it stops, the rod bends, then jerks the lure forward. It then shoots ahead and momentarily pauses until the slack line catches up with the rod tip. Whether super-aggressive or just following, a fish can easily open his mouth while he catches up with the temporarily slowed lure and inhale it.

Another method for "luring" fish that may not be hitting super hot, hitting short or not hitting at all is trolling a pattern. Some "experts" claim the best trolling formula is one that requires a college algebra course to compute. I suggest trolling in lazy "S" turns. When you turn to the left, the inside lures will slow down. This allows the neutral fish time to react. When you turn back to the right again, the lures on the right slow down. The pattern becomes very clear.

Most trollers have noticed the effects of the "S" pattern before. For example, when you make rapid course changes to go back across your fish, the inside rod often catches a fish. That's not an accident. Some anglers do this by sweeping their rod tip six feet forward then dropping the tip back. This stop-and-go lure action can be very successful.

The change in action caused by a speed-up or slow-down often triggers fish. More importantly, the speed change permits non-aggressive or neutral fish (those not actively seeking their next meal) time to react and inhale the crankbait, a morsel that intruded into their "space," stopped, surged forward and paused again. This makes it easy for a fish to eat with a minimal amount of energy. I've discovered that slowing down rather than speeding up triggers more fish. Periodically, shift to neutral for as long as 20 to 30 seconds. When the boat slows to less that one mile per hour, floaters will rise slowly and the sinking lures will descend towards bottom. Remember the boat will still be coasting ahead and a following fish can grab an easy meal. This is especially effective on calm days.

HOW CAN I CATCH MORE FISH TROLLING?

Depth is the key! Trolling lures to catch fish is an ancient style of fishing. We take this technique for granted, but it was probably developed about the same time man floated his first boat. Perhaps a paddle or the wind provided the power to drag a bait through the water. Then fishing boats with oars became the rage, as they still are in many parts of the world.

After oars came outboard motors, which really kicked trolling into high gear. The outboard did the work allowing fishermen to concentrate on trolling speeds, lure action and pulling the lures where they wanted. Early trolling was done by familiarization with a small section of a lake (or by guesswork), because fishermen had no way of measuring depth. They certainly didn't know if fish were suspended between the surface and the bottom. Modern day trolling began simply enough with three-way swivels, drop sinkers and lures or baits trolled close to the bottom. The weight on the sinker became a depth finder when it came in contact with the bottom. It was also the depth control gauge. Depth was not controlled, but followed. Lures would rise and fall with the bottom contour. There was no real need at this early stage of trolling to know the depths that lures ran. However, with the advent of electronics, quantum leaps in trolling have taken place.

The reasons for trolling remain the same for fishing in any body of water: 1) a maximum amount of water can be covered in a limited time; 2) generally, larger fish hit trolled crankbaits; 3) contact (lure presentation) can be made to more fish, increasing the odds of triggering an inactive fish or finding an aggressive fish; and, 4) scattered fish are generally active and can be located quickest by trolling than any other method.

Fishermen can now run lures through fish on the bottom as they always done, or they can try for suspended fish. They can troll alongside structure or weeds, or anyplace fish show up on electronics. Remember, the depth a crankbait runs still holds the key to reaching fish.

Even though fishermen debate everyday the merits of color and the shape of lures, these concerns are secondary. In my opinion, nothing else is important unless you can get a lure to the fish. To do this, you must have a knowledge of depth.

Many times I've been fishing within a pack of boats, all drifting ahead of a good breeze. Everybody was covering water when all of a sudden the wind died. Trolling became the order of the day, yet almost every time, 90 percent of the fishermen would spend most of the day trying to "make" their lures run at the right depth. Their methods ranged from choosing their favorite lures to just putting one on and trolling. The lures either ran someplace off the bottom or hung-up when they bumped the bottom. If they didn't catch fish (after 15 or 20 minutes), depth or color was blamed, and the fishermen would switch to yet another lure.

Most of the anglers neither found the correct depth nor developed the confidence gained from knowledge; they had known the fish were a foot off the bottom. After all, they'd been catching the fish at that depth earlier while drifting. Their only method of learning lure depth was trial and error. When they caught a fish, if they caught one, their test was successful. But they still weren't quite sure why. Was it depth? If they had hit upon the correct depth, would another style of lure running at the same depth at a different speed work better? Because they didn't know the original reason for catching fish, they couldn't experiment to find the most effective tactics or lures.

Knowing the exact depth each lure runs eliminates trial and error. Only when you know the exact trolling range can you immediately select a lure for the fish.

Once in the fish zone, the only experimenting is then with colors or lure styles. If you want to troll fast, you must know which lures to use for a particular speed. When you want to troll slow, the models which run at a specific depth at a slow speed should be selected. If trolling in a circle (say you're patrolling the area around an island or underwater hump), run a "slow" lure on the inside and a "fast" lure on the outside. If the fish are foraging on a certain size minnow, you should use a lure that matches the size and shape of that bait and run at, or slightly above, the depth of the fish.

Knowing the lure's depth will help increase your catch; it's a simple matter of arithmetic. Having your bait spend more time where the fish are will easily produce more fish.

TROUBLE-SHOOTING TIP

Eliminate Guesswork

The "Crankbait Depth Guide & Calculator" eliminates guesswork so that you can start fishing 200 individual lures in their fish zones.

The days of throwing a lure behind the boat and randomly dragging it across the lake is history. If you want to be successful, you must locate fish, know their depth, choose a lure that runs at that depth, then begin your trolling plan. You'll be attacking the situation efficiently. When you're where the fish are and a fish can strike your lure, you're fishing; the rest of the time, you're only *going fishing*.

A copy of the "Crankbait Depth Guide & Calculator" can be purchased from Fishing Enterprises, P.O. Box 7108, Pierre, SD 57501. Or call 1-800-223-9126.

174 WALLEYE TROUBLE-SHOOTING

Gary Parsons is the master of trolling techniques.

WHEN SHOULD YOU USE TROLLING BOARDS?

This question seems so simple, yet you could write an entire book on the subject. As a matter of fact, my friend Gary Parsons has done just that. Along with being one of the top tournament fishermen on the professional circuit, Gary has been a pioneer and an innovator of the uses of many types of trolling systems. So why not ask the expert? I did and this is his answer:

Actually, this is a surprisingly simple question to answer. You want to use boards whenever you feel that walleyes are feeding close to the surface. This minimizes the 'boat spooking' factor while trolling. Another time to use boards is during trolling procedures where adding lines will increase the mathematical odds of contacting fish. Of course in each situation, you want to be in a relatively snag-free area or using boards can become too much of a hassle.

I couldn't agree more with Gary. The hard part of trolling is keeping it simple and not over-thinking it. Whenever you have scattered fish, planer boards will allow the spreading of lines to cover more area and put the baits past more fish. This coupled with the ability to add additional lines greatly increases your fish-catching odds.

What type of planer board to use will depend a great deal on the type of water you're fishing. For example, if you're on suspended walleyes in big, open water (such as Lake Erie), you may want to use a mast and ski system. The system allows you to expand on your presentation by using snap-on weights to take lures deeper. You might also use lead-core or wire lines.

If you're on a lake that requires more precision trolling, you'll want to use an in-line planer board. This board attaches to each individual line and can perform the same duties as the ski and mast system. The planer board is very effective for precision trolling around and along structure.

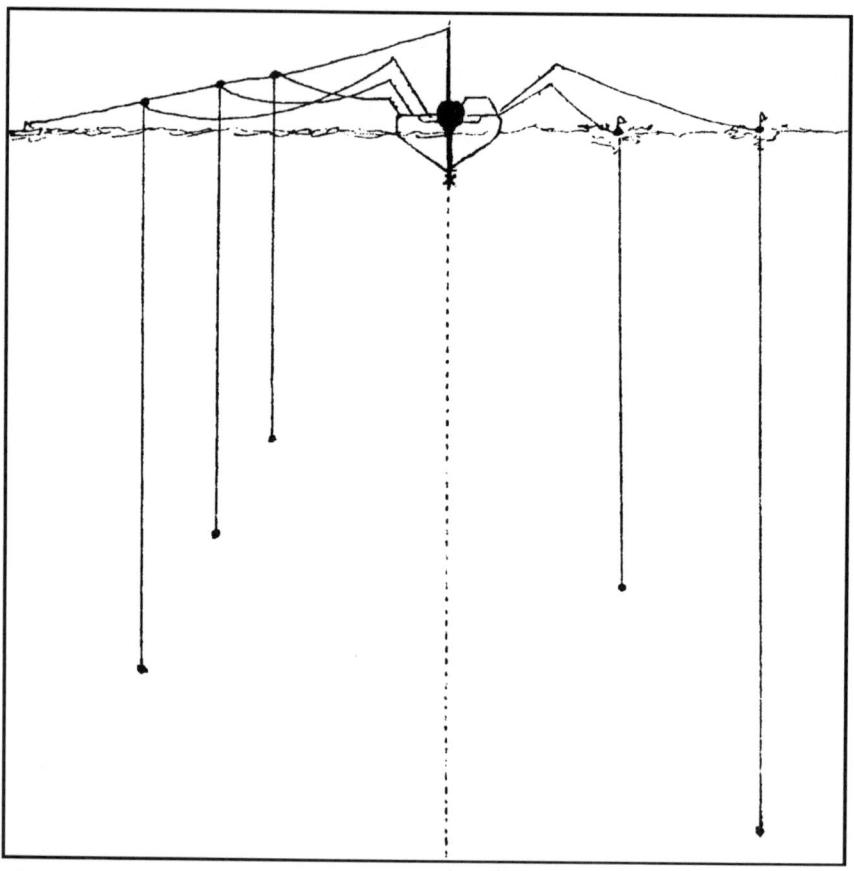

Spreading out your lines is done two ways: The left side of the boat is a mast with skis and the right side with planer boards.

Although there are many different styles and types of in-line planer boards on the market, there's one that is outstanding. It's the Off-Shore planer board. It not only pulls the baits better, but it's quick and easy to use. Consider nothing else!

QUESTION 41   **WHEN SHOULD YOU USE**   177
                                                   TROLLING BOARDS?

Now, back to the main question: "When do I use trolling boards?" Whenever you're trolling and say to yourself, "I wonder if I should put on a planer board?" Do it! Keep it simple and don't over think it. Add some simple techniques such as changing boat speed by slowing down or speeding up which can often trigger a hit. My preferred method of speed fluctuation is to simply troll in a series of "S" turns. This will speed up the outside baits and slow down the inside baits.

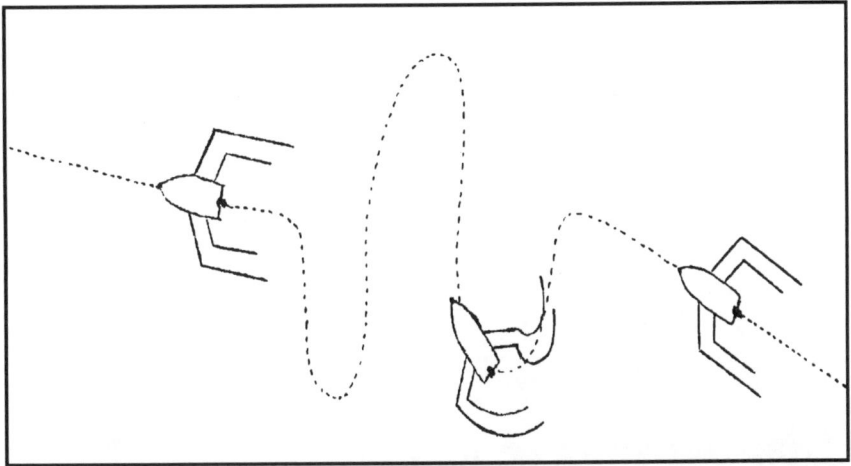

Using "S" turns as a trolling pattern will speed up the outside baits and slow down the inside baits, which often triggers a hit.

Whatever type of trolling system you use, remember the goal is to put the odds in your favor, especially with scattered or spooky fish. Use your imagination; change depths, speed, color, and styles of baits.

By the way, there's just one more thing to make your trolling system more effective and your life much simpler: "Troll with the wind, not against it."

WHAT'S THE KEY TO CASTING CRANKBAITS?

The skill of casting a crankbait isn't dependent on how far you can throw it. What's more important is where the bait lands and what happens when that bait is underwater. Presenting the lure to the fish means retrieving as close as possible to the same depth of the fish. For example, when casting to a steep bank, select a quick diving crankbait which will run parallel to the sloping bottom. If you're fishing from the bank, reach for a crankbait like a Rattl'n Spot or another sinking lure. Cast it out, count it down to the proper depth (about one foot per second), or let it hit bottom, then retrieve it up from the deep. The lure will follow the fish-holding structure from deep water to your toes. Always relate crankbaits to the area being fished. It's not how many casts you make in a day but,

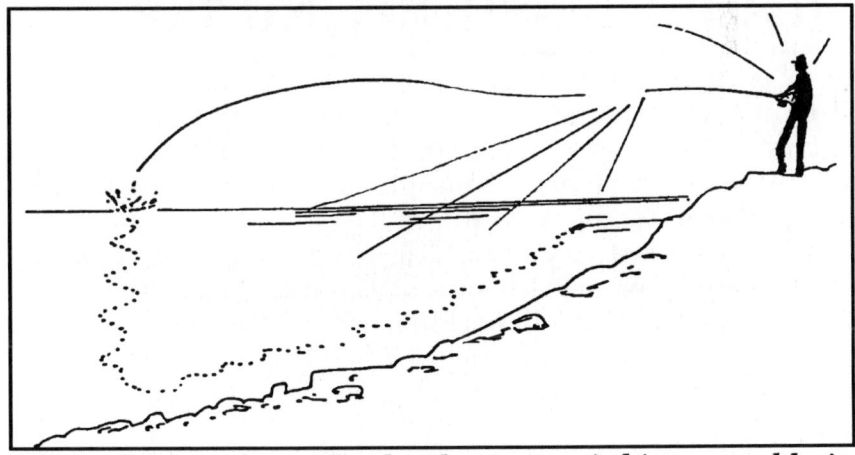

When fishing from the bank use a sinking crankbait. Cast it out and count it down until you feel it's at the proper depth. As you retrieve your bait it will parallel the slope of the structure, keeping you in the fish zone.

rather it's how effectively you present your lure to the most fish in every situation. For example, if fish are scattered on a shallow flat, you need a shallow running bait and one which can be cast a long distance. When fishing shallow water, always try to cast with the wind to achieve the greatest distance. You'll never cast far enough away from the boat if you're positioned incorrectly or throwing against the wind.

In shallow water, fish the fish before you scare them. Shallow, clear water means long casts. This can be accomplished with several lures, such as the Rattlin' Spot. These half-ounce sinking lures are dense and offer very little wind resistance which in turn means longer casts. Depth can be controlled by retrieval speed, line diameter and the amount of time the lure is allowed to sink before retrieving. Through trial and error, you'll determine the speed and depth ratio. These lures can then be "ripped" through weeds which often triggers strikes. For shallow water with rocks, weeds or a combination, I like the Rebel Minnow, a lightweight floater. It catches the wind and really sails. Its retrieval depth is just under

---

TROUBLE-SHOOTING TIP

Tune Every Lure And Here's How:

To tune a crankbait to run straight, bend the line-attaching eye in the opposite direction that it's running. Always start with slight adjustments and keep testing. Use a needle nose pliers.

(a) For lures with eyelet in lip, bend the eyelet slightly and evenly toward the side of the lip. Cast, retrieve, and test until the lure is perfect.

(b) For lures with metal lips and connecting link, use your fingers to bend the link in the middle. Don't bend the lip!

(c) For lures with an eyelet in the nose, grasp the eyelet with a pliers and very carefully bend the eyelet. Small adjustments are a must and should be constantly fine-tuned.

the surface, allowing you to fish shallow, rocky areas. Remember, even when you've matched the crankbait to the correct depth, fish aren't always suicidal and "attack" your lure.

To increase your success per retrieve, fish so that the fish can eat. One simple tactic is to pull the rod tip up a few feet, pause, pick-up the slack and repeat. After each pull the lure slows and becomes motionless for a brief period of time. This allows a fish the reaction time necessary to suck in the crankbait easily, whether he's on a feeding spree or not.

A neutral buoyant crankbait (one that doesn't float or sink) works best for the "stop-and-go" retrieve. After reeling it down, the lure hits its maximum depth and stays there while twitched back. Rob Kilby, Hot Springs, Arkansas, a top BASS tournament pro, makes his Rebel Floating Minnow crankbaits neutral buoyant by adding small split shot to the body cavity. By adding enough weight to a floating bait so that it doesn't sink or float, he is able to pull his lure a few feet, stop it, and give the fish time to react. Since many strikes occur on slack line, sharp hooks are vital.

TROUBLE-SHOOTING TIP
Casting Shallow Water Walleyes

Casting crankbaits is a very effective presentation for shallow water walleyes, especially if you work them with a stop-and-go retrieve. Choose a crankbait that is as close as possible to neutral. After casting, crank your bait into the depth you want and then retrieve it with three-foot strokes of the rod. Do this by pulling the rod tip three or four feet back to take up the slack. Continue this all the way back to the boat. This system works great on a break where shallow water turns deep or at the edge of a weed line. A crankbait that's neutral buoyant, like a suspending Rogue, works fine. Cast it out and retrieve it back in three or four-foot jerks.

Often fish will be active only on the lip of a drop-off and a cast over this zone will bring a lure through it (stop-n-go) and give the fish time to react. Any series of twitches can be utilized, but the rule to follow is: short jerks in cool weather, more emphatic in warm weather. In other words, crankbaits must be "fished," not just cast and retrieved.

On a weed line, be sure to cast and crank from the shallow water to the inside edge of the weeds. Stop the floating lure at the weed edge and watch for a bulge in the line as the stalled lure disappears. To continue reeling would mean weed-fouled hooks. This opportunity on the inside weed edge is ignored by many fishermen and seldom fished by crankbait anglers.

WHEN DO YOU FISH A BOTTOM BOUNCER?

A bottom bouncer should be in the heart of your walleye arsenal. You'll find that bottom bouncer fishing is fun, easy, and the whole family can do it.

Whether drifting or trolling, simply remember to let out enough line so that the bottom bouncer touches bottom. Fish the bottom bouncer by keeping track of the bottom and remember, speed is important. If using spinners, go fast enough so that the spinner blade spins. If the spinner doesn't spin, it will snag. When your speed is not fast enough for a spinner to spin, use a plain hook or tie a crankbait on three to four feet behind the bottom bouncer.

I fish the bottom bouncer three ways. The first method I use, about 10 percent of the time, employs a crank-

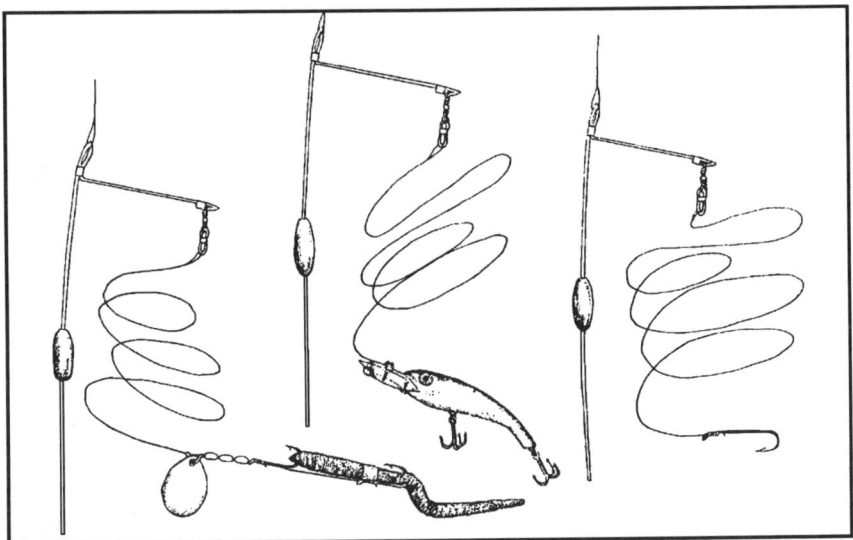

Bottom bouncers allow a variety of bait presentations.

bait. I tie a shallow diving crankbait like a Rebel Minnow to the the bottom bouncer with a four to five-foot leader when fishing vertical structure. No other presentation allows a crankbait to run a foot off the bottom in 10 feet, down to 30 feet and up to 10 feet again. Generally, you'll find the biggest fish on the steepest structure, whether it's along the side or on the tip where the point drops into deeper water.

The second method I use is with a spinner, which I use about 20 percent of the time. This is a top producer in big wind and waves on flats. When drifting, all I have to do is drop the spinner over the side and make sure the wind is blowing the boat fast enough for the blade to spin. The big waves seem to trigger aggressive fish looking for movement.

Method three, used in about 70 percent of my total bottom bouncer fishing, is done with a single hook on a

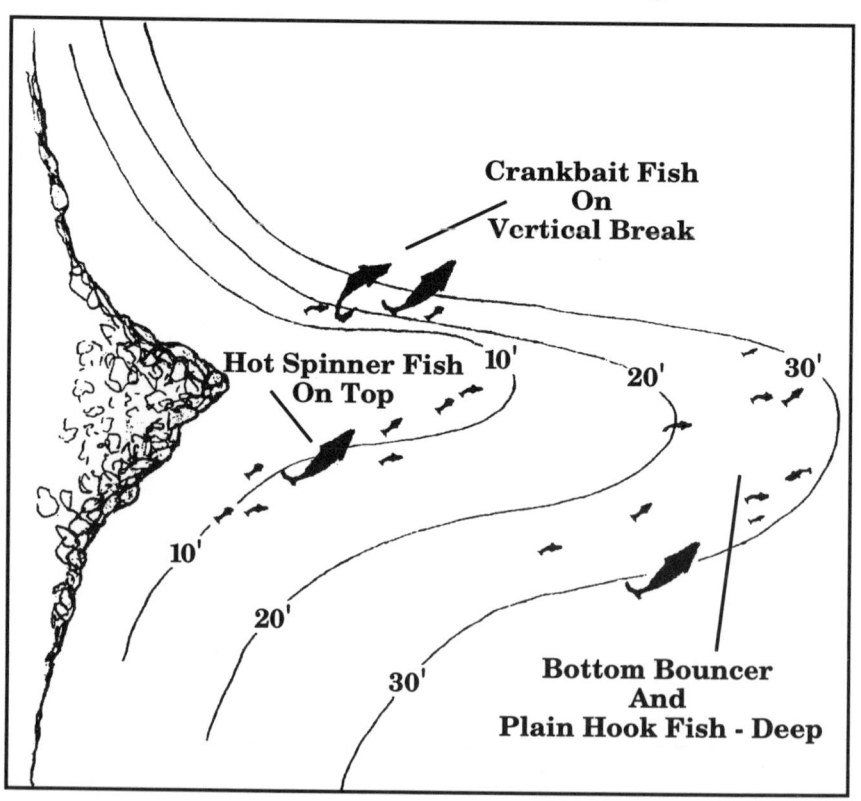

TROUBLE-SHOOTING TIP

Eliminate Short Hits

Pulling a bottom bouncer through the water at a steady pace has a tendency to cause walleyes to short-hit. Walleyes have a habit of following just behind the bait, then they'll try to suck in the bait as they inhale the water that surrounds it. Needless to say, your tight line doesn't allow this natural feeding process to take place and creats a short-hit.

The remedy for short hits is simple. Use multiple-hooks on spinners and worm harnesses. On straight hook rigs, place a small styrofoam float in the center of your leader. By floating the center of the leader, you create the slack between the weight and the bait. This will allow the bait to flow backwards into the walleye's mouth as he inhales.

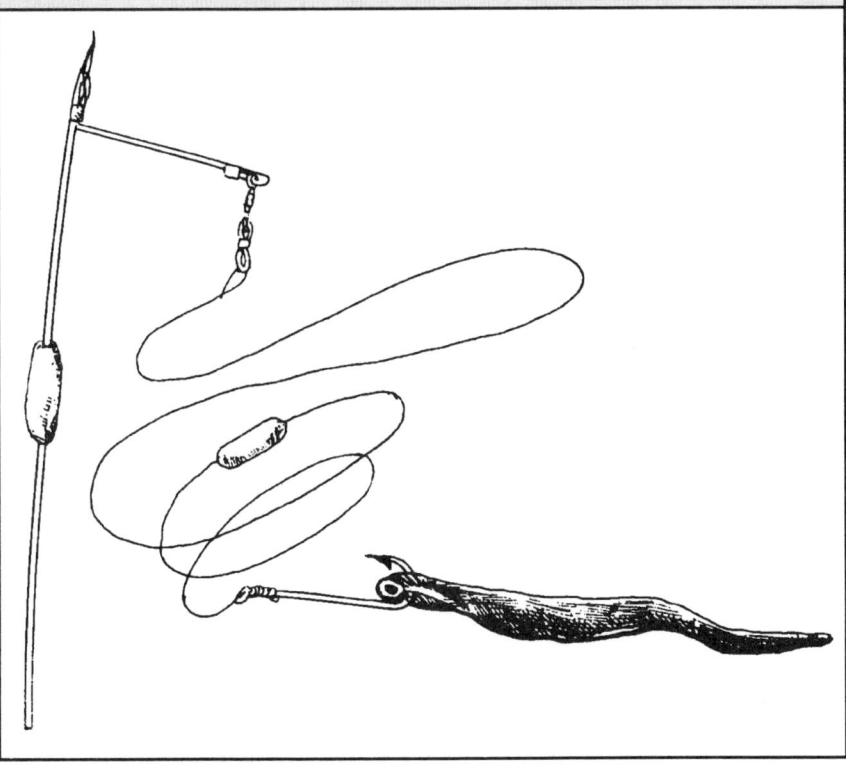

four to five-foot leader with a #1 or #2 Aberdeen light wire hook. I can bait this with a minnow, leech or crawler. Hook the minnow through the lips, the crawler throughout the middle (not through the head), and the leech near the sucker. The leech is my favorite bait because it's durable, lives a long time and swims continually. Fish the plain hook anytime the boat isn't moving fast enough for a blade to spin, or use this system anytime you're fishing an area over 30 feet deep. When you're over 30 feet deep, you'll have some difficulty keeping the bottom bouncer down, while still moving fast enough to keep a spinner spinning.

The bottom bouncer is not a magic bait, but it sure seems like it. Jerry Anderson, one of the nation's top walleye fishermen, from Onamia, Minnesota, summed it up best when he said, "A bottom bouncer works better than it should."

HOW DO YOU FISH JIGS?

The formula for jig fishing success is simple. Don't over-fish them and don't make it difficult. One of the most attractive features of jig fishing is its ease of use. Often touted as difficult, demanding fine-tuned expensive rods and needing years of practice, jig fishing is actually easy. Anyone can do it. With the right attitude, jig fishing is the simplest and most fun presentation I know.

> ## TROUBLE-SHOOTING TIP
> ### The Jig Is Up
> Anglers have a tendency to shy away from jigs. They think that it's a technique only used by experts, that it takes 20 years to develop a sensitive touch, and the purchase of a $300 ultra-sensitive rod - WRONG! Jigging is easy. You can jig with a broomstick and do it well the first time out!

The proper attitude for jig fishing success is also simple; it consists of two rules:

1) Use your jig simply to keep track of the bottom whether drifting, trolling, casting or vertical jigging. Simply lift the jig off the bottom and drop it back down until it touches. Repeat this action and remember: keep track of the bottom.

2) Forget about trying to *make* a fish bite, forget about trying to *feel* a hit. Simply keep track of the bottom and set the hook if you feel anything different. Set the hook if you think you're snagged, set the hook if you feel a tick, set the hook if you thought you felt *anything*

Mike holds a "bonus fish" which come frequently while jigging.

at all. Always set the hook. It costs nothing and you'll be amazed how often those suspicions of what could have been a fish, turn into one.

Just follow these two suggestions; 1) keep track of the bottom, and 2) set the hook whenever you feel anything. Do this and you'll become an accomplished jig fisherman on your first day on the water.

With a little practice, jigs can open up a whole new world in fishing. You'll learn to read depths by the length of time it takes your jig to settle to the bottom. You'll be able to feel a hump or the slightest drop-off. You'll learn to map in your mind the shape of an underwater structure and mentally paint an underwater picture. A complete mental picture with drop-offs, angles, weeds, rocks and fish location can happen for you.

Attitude Adjustment

I suggest that you make an attitude adjustment from the very start. Don't try to *make* fish bite. Instead develop an attitude of keeping in contact with the bottom. This will ensure maximum "drop" in as near a vertical position as possible. Allow the fish to eat and don't try to make them bite. This attitude will also keep your presentation close to structure where fish are more likely to be lurking.

Learn To See The Jig Hit Bottom

My advice is to concentrate on watching the line as the jig falls. When the jig hits bottom, the line will go limp and collapse. This is the best way to recognize if your jig is where you want it to be, on the bottom. When a fish hits, the line will not go limp on the fall. This "sight strike" is far easier to recognize than trying to feel the "thunk" every time your jig drops.

Set The Hook When You Feel Anything

One of the most challenging things when jig fishing is to forget about trying to differentiate between a snag and a fish. If something solid registers on your line, set the hook immediately. Find out quickly if it's bottom or a fish. If you are hesitant, it gives the fish time to spit out the hook. Always set the hook because many times a snag feels like a fish, and a fish feels like a snag.

Recognize When It's Time To Jig

The time to fish jigs is when walleyes are holding tight, bunched up in a small area or concentrated along contour or depth. Jigging should not be used to work over scattered fish or to find fish. Jigging is usually at its best when you've located fish and you need longevity in your presentation.

Put Color In Its Place

Does color make a difference? I'm not a fan of color. If others are catching fish in the boat and you're not, you'd be wise to observe the *action* that's being used on their jigs. Color selection has been used as a scapegoat for being responsible for presenting the right bait in the best possible manner. This is not true! It's how you work the jig. The *action* of the jig is highly significant. In fact only *attitude* and *concentration* rank higher. The key to action with a jig is making it do what you want it to do. You can twitch it, hop it, drag it, or just let it sit there. The real key is being able to repeat what has been successful.

WHEN DO YOU USE A LINDY RIG?

As with any presentation, the rules never change; location dictates presentation. The following are the location keys that tell me when a Lindy rig should be used:

Deep water: Anything over 20 feet.

Calm windless conditions: This allows precision boat control and exact presentation on tightly schooled fish near structure.

Clean bottom areas: A clean bottom is necessary as you'll be dragging your weight on it. If the bottom is too snaggy, change your Lindy weight to a Lite Bite bottom bouncer system.

Tightly schooled fish: Tightly schooled fish near structure usually aren't on the bite. Remember, they need time to react to a bait. Always present your Lindy rig as slowly as possible.

Specific pieces of structure: Structure that is holding fish near the bottom at a uniform depth such as submerged weed lines, shelves, or stair steps on underwater structure calls for a Lindy rig.

Any one of these keys can be a signal for you to consider a Lindy rig. Many times all of these keys can be present at the same time, and a Lindy rig is the order of the day.

Although the Lindy rig is an important piece in the foundation of walleye fishing, it too is susceptible to change. Just as knowledge and new materials have changed; steel fishing rods to fiberglass and then to graphite, the Lindy rig has also evolved. Today, we now call it the Roach rig.

With the Roach rig, snell adjustment is a must. You have to present the bait where the fish are. For exam-

> **TROUBLE-SHOOTING TIP**
>
> ### Roach Rig
> The Roach rig is a Lindy rig with the added advantage of instantly being able to adjust your leader length. By using a rubber bobber stop on the line in place of a swivel, it can slip up and down your line, lengthening or shortening your snell.

ple, you notice on your electronics that the fish have lifted a few feet off the bottom. Don't continue to drag your bait on the bottom. Lengthen your leader, add a small styrofoam float to the leader, or blow your nightcrawler full of air. This will float your bait up to the same level as the fish. The longer the leader length, the higher the bait will float. This adjustment can be done instantly with a Roach rig.

Just as important as when to use a Lindy rig is when *not* to use one. A Lindy rig can be a deadly method of

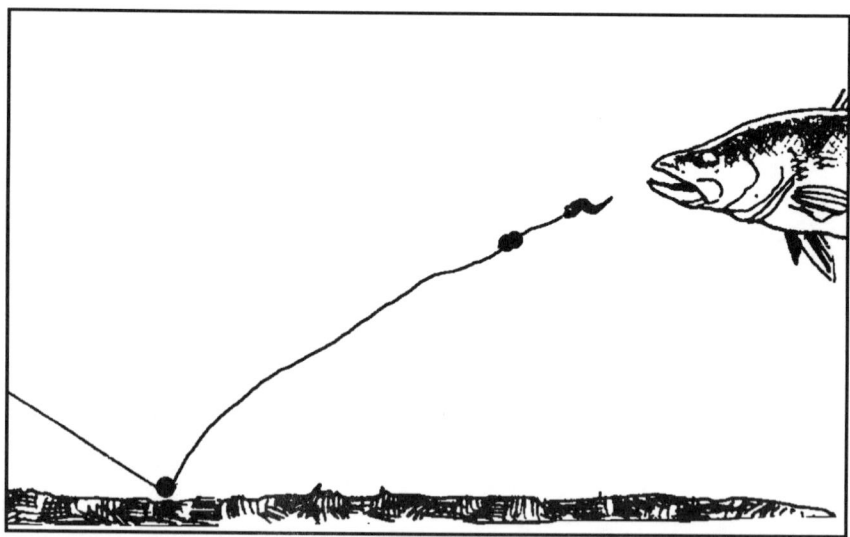

Snell adjustment on your Lindy rig allows you to catch those fish that have raised off the bottom. Lengthen your leader and add a small styrofoam float.

catching fish, literally. Anytime you hook a fish deep in the throat or in the stomach, severe damage is done. Even with the greatest care in removing the hook or clipping the line and leaving the hook, the fish's chances of survival are slim. Instead, use a quick strike method. Simply make an adjustment in your presentation that will allow a walleye to inhale the bait and hook successfully on the first try. This is done by creating slack between the bait and the weight. The slack will allow the entire bait and hook to move with the flow of

TROUBLE-SHOOTING TIP

Quick Strike System

If you know you'll be keeping every walleye you catch, the Lindy rig system is fine. But, if you cull small fish (replacing a smaller fish in your live well with a larger one), or release large fish, don't let them swallow the hook. Use a quick strike method of Lindy

water into the fish's mouth.

There are two simple ways to rig for a quick strike presentation. The first is to simply tie a small Styrofoam float to the center of your leader, creating the slack that's necessary for the fish to inhale the entire bait and hook on the first try.

The second method for a quick strike rig is to use a coiled leader. This is a leader made of line you have

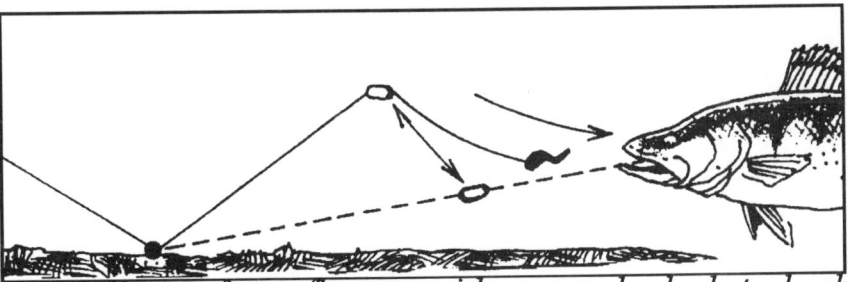

A small styrofoam float provides enough slack to hook into the fish's mouth on the first try.

stripped from an old reel and retains its memory. The gentle coil also provides the slack needed to successfully hook a fish as soon as you feel him hit.

A coiled leader provides the slack needed to hook a fish as soon as you feel a hit.

As more state fishing regulations adopt size and slot limits for walleyes, requiring the release of certain sizes of fish, the use of quick strike rigging systems becomes more and more a requirement of a healthy fishing industry.

WHEN SHOULD I USE BOBBERS?

Bobbers (or floats) are an important part of any walleye fisherman's tackle presentation. Bobbers and slip bobber angling is geared to present a bait to a small, specific target area at a specific depth. For this reason bobbers are obviously the equipment of choice for fishing weeds, trees, or rocky edges of reefs.

TROUBLE-SHOOTING TIP
Fishing Shallow Reefs
Slip bobbers come into their own as a top technique when waves are crashing over the tops of shallow reefs. Walleyes use the diffused light caused by the waves to their advantage as they can see better than their prey. A jig tipped with a crawler, leech or minnow under a bobber should be set to keep it close to the bottom. Weight the float enough so that it doesn't bob up with the waves but let the waves wash over it. This smooth presentation, rather than one being bounced by the waves, seems to be preferred by walleyes as it offers them an easier meal.

Fish a bobber on cold, non-aggressive fish that are tightly schooled. This allows maximum presentation time to trigger a bite even if the fish aren't actively seeking food. Remember, once a fish is caught, pay attention! Cast the bobber back to exactly the same spot at the same depth. On the flip side, never cast twice to the same spot until fish are located.

Using a seven-foot spinning rod for bobbers will work

the best. A long rod that absorbs shock while maintaining tension works well with light line. The length of the rod also gives you the ability to remove line slack when setting the hook. Because you're using light line (four to six pound test on long rods), jigs and hooks must be small. I like a round headed 1/16 or 1/8 ounce jig with the eye on top or a #6 or #8 hook with a light split-shot attached above the hook.

TROUBLE-SHOOTING TIP

Save Your Bobber

In "snaggy" areas where heavier line is necessary, tie a slip bobber knot above and below the float. This will save the bobber when you catch an occasional snag.

Bobber action is usually provided by the wind, but on calm days, don't let the bobber sit. Try jigging, jerking, twitching, anything to move it every 30 seconds or so.

Of all baits to use when fishing bobbers, leeches are by far the winner. On calm days leeches wiggle, almost inviting a walleye to eat them! A healthy leech's durability is unmatched. It allows long casts while avoiding the hassle of inadvertently tossing the bait off and having to reel in time and time again. The worst thing that can happen is fishing a hook without bait!

Knowing when *not* to use bobbers is very important. Scattered fish on a flat can be fished with other methods that work better and faster. Aggressive fish will easily hit bobbers, but when time is a factor, a jig will out-fish bobbers when the "bite is on." Deep fish over 25 feet are the poorest choice for bobber fishing. It just takes too long for the bait to reach the bottom, and deep fish are usually scattered.

Remember, you don't have to just sit and stare at your bobber all day. Bobbers will work with other presentations such as casting a jig or crankbait. Try to place the bobber in a position that's easy to see and won't interfere with casting. The bobber will present a bait better to fish which aren't actively feeding than a jig. The opposite applies for the jig which seeks out those aggressive fish that may be roaming in the area.

By using the jig and bobber presentations at the same time, you'll not only increase the fish-catching odds, but you will also avoid being bored while waiting for the bobber to disappear.

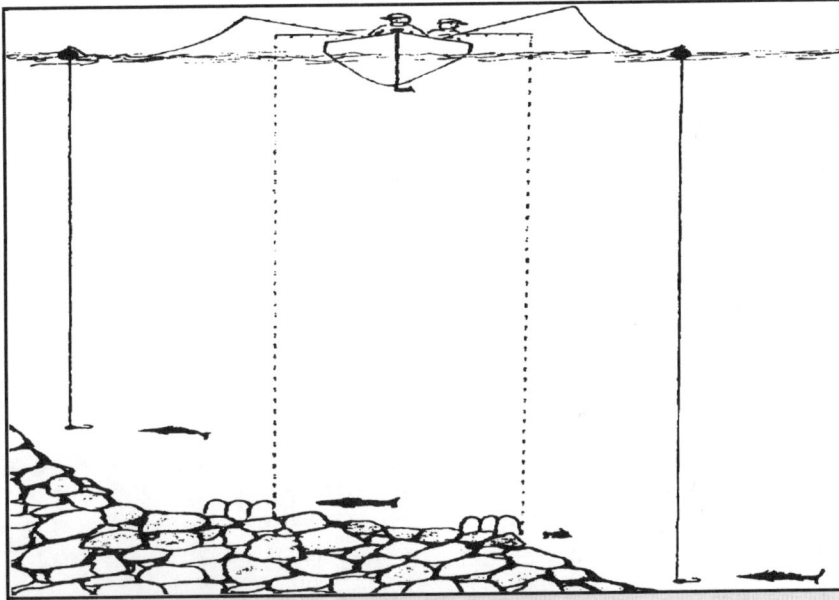

TROUBLE-SHOOTING TIP

Missing Fish On Bobbers?

A coiled leader (a leader made from used line that retains its coiled memory when stripped from the reel) of four to six-pound test line will solve this problem.

The soft coil of line will draw the hook back to the weight and create the slack necessary for the fish to gently inhale the bait with the flow of water being sucked in by the walleye through his gills.

When the bobber disappears, set the hook. You'll find the entire bait and hook were drawn into the fish's mouth.

South Dakota Tourism Photo

HOW DO YOU FISH CURRENT FROM THE BANK?

That's a tough question and just one of the concerns of many who fish from the bank. Being a professional tournament fisherman, the vast majority of my time is spent in a boat. As a professional lecturer on fishing, I realize the majority of the fishing questions are "from the bank." There are so many questions that my next book will be directed at bank fishermen and titled <u>Bank Fishing Secrets.</u>

As for now I'll plead ignorance and turn this question over to an expert, Jack McClelland. Along with being a top tournament pro, Jack is also a full-time guide on the Missouri River below Oahe Dam. Although much of his fishing is from a boat, he has spent many days and nights guiding clients from the bank and can offer valuable insights to solving the question of fishing current from the shore. Jack is also my brother, and here's his answer:

The first thing you need to consider is what tackle do you need? Here's a list of tackle with which you'll want to start with:

* *A rod that can be used for casting crankbaits and jigs.*
* *A longer rod (eight to nine feet) suitable for walking baits along the shore.*
* *An assortment of jigs, plastic bodies and Rapala floaters, count-downs, or homemade neutral buoyant type lures.*
* *A dip-net that is semi-snag free for fishing crankbaits at night.*

Since much of current bank fishing will take place at night, a good light source for rigging, netting or unhooking fish is critical. This light source can be either a flashlight or lantern, but the best that I have found is a headlamp. A headlamp is a hands-free light that is worn on the head and used by miners and/or people that work at night and use both hands.

You'll need a pair of needle nose pliers or a large set of forceps for unhooking the catch. I carry both of these with me at all times. I like to use the forceps because I can lock them to my jacket when not in use, and they're easily accessible. I carry the needle nose pliers because they have a cutter built into them, and I may have to straighten a hook or cut off a barb if the bait becomes snagged in the net, clothing, or any part of my body.

TROUBLE-SHOOTING TIP

Use Chap-Stick

Much of your bank fishing will be done in the spring and fall. Some of your fishing time will be in temperatures well below freezing. To keep the ice from freezing your rod eye-lets closed, simply apply chap-stick.

As far as what is the best technique and what are the best baits for the bank, there are many. The key consideration is a bait that's neutral buoyant. Neutral buoyant means the bait won't sink or float, but just suspends in the water like a fish! Fish are neutral buoyant and that means baitfish are neutral buoyant! Try to duplicate this knowledge with your crankbaits. First of all you need to alter your crankbait by placing the lead from a .22 caliber shell into the body of the lure. Another way to achieve neutrality is the use of lead tape. This can be purchased at nearly any well-stocked bait or tackle shop. To use this form of weight, attach it to the underside of the bait.

I personally like to use a bait that is slightly less than neutral buoyant when fishing currents and rip-rap known as "lure-eating rocks." When the lure is hung up in the rocks, try not to become excited and set the hook. After a few such encounters, you'll be able to distinguish

QUESTION 47 — HOW DO YOU FISH CURRENT FROM THE BANK?

When fishing from shore, don't be species-orientated. Take advantage of whatever fish are available.

between a fish and a snag. If the lure does become snagged, slack up the line and move down the shore in the direction of the lure if possible. Most of the time, your lure will be hung up less than four feet from shore and being less than neutral buoyant, the current will help float out and save your bait.

When fishing the current, look for the changes that will be most evident such as eddies and small breaks with slack water behind them, a current seam, small indents, pockets, or bends along the rip-rap. These will be the places where walleyes can tuck in away from the current and ambush any bait that comes along.

As far as presentation, always consider the current and natural flow of the walleye's food. Jigs should be cast upstream at about a 45-degree angle and retrieved with a jigging motion. The weight of the jig you use will be decided by the strength of the current being fished.

Crankbaits should be cast at a 90-degree angle to the shore and retrieved slowly. Even after the bait has seemingly come around the bank, continue to slowly retrieve it all the way to the shore. Most of your hits will be within three feet of the shore, and many will be right at your feet.

The long rod that I suggested is used to walk baits up the shoreline, conditions permitting. I also use the long rod to hold a bait in one spot in the current or break seam.

No matter what time of the year that you fish, remember the most important thing is to find out all you can about the area being fished. What works at that particular time of the year and in that location is what will constitute your 'angling plan.'

I guess fishing the current from the bank isn't much different from boat fishing. Communicating with other anglers and sharing the information is still the key to success - along with a smile.

WHAT'S THE BEST WAY TO CATCH WALLEYES IN WEEDS?

Once walleyes are found in weeds, choosing the best presentation can be quite a frustrating experience. Remember to always choose a presentation that can put the odds in your favor and not one that's merely your favorite way to fish. Let's look at several different methods of presentation and the circumstances you would choose for each.

Bottom Bouncers & Spinners

Bottom bouncers are not considered by most anglers as a presentation in weeds, but they remain one of the most effective for me. A bottom bouncer can fish weed edges faster than any other presentation. The trick is to

Weed edges are the ideal place for walleyes to ambush their lunch. Weeds not only offer cover to conceal walleyes, they form a natural barrier that channels migrating schools of baitfish.

fish a particular depth, not the weeds. Begin by identifying the depth at which the weeds are no longer growing (the weed edge). Weed growth is dictated by light penetration into the water. In other words, if you find weeds have stopped growing at nine feet of water depth, it means that the underwater weed edge is nine feet on the entire lake. Now that the weed edge has been established, simply use your depth finder to pull the bottom bouncer in 10 feet of water. This depth will be close to the weeds, yet clear of them. This is the perfect spot for a walleye lying in cover ready to ambush dinner as he's traveling along the clean edge of the weeds.

Crankbaits

A crankbait is effective when cast along a weed edge; however, a crankbait does its best when cast over new weed growth. The crankbait's advantage isn't only in the tremendous amount of area it can cover, but its ability to run at a particular depth.

Crankbaits allow fishing weeds at any uniform depth. For example, if weeds have grown three feet off the bottom in 12 feet of water, choose a Wally Diver; it will just clear the weed tops at eight feet on a long cast. On a return trip to these weeds a week or so later, you'll find the weeds may have grown to five or six feet off the bottom, choose a new lure that once again just clears the tops of the weeds.

Locating new underwater weeds can be challenging. The simplest way is to note where the weeds are when they are fully grown and lying on the surface in August.

TROUBLE-SHOOTING TIP

Finding Underwater Weed Depths

Finding the depth on new weed growth below the water is simply done by increasing your depth with different crankbaits. Once you've hit the weeds, simply choose the crankbait that ran a little higher.

These areas will produce weeds year after year. Make notes or use a GPS so you can return to the exact area in the spring. This will allow you to fish the weeds throughout their entire growing cycle.

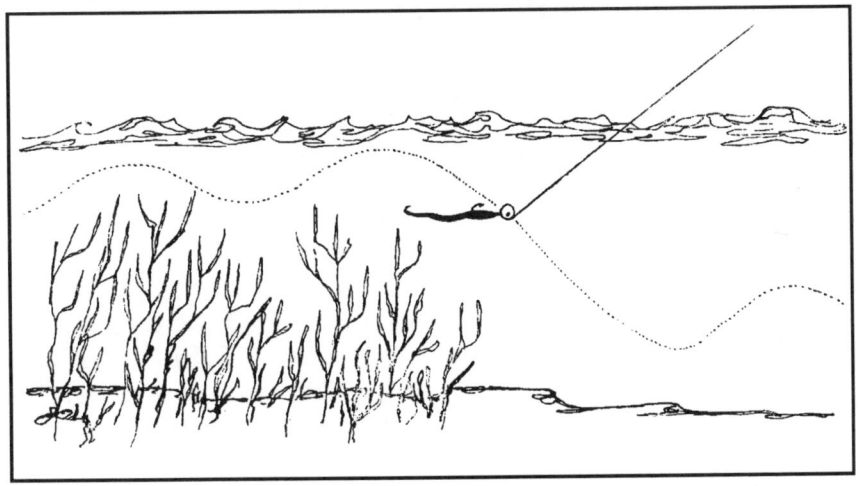

By slowly swimming your jig with a tight line, you can fish just over the tops of weeds at any depths.

Jigs

Jigging is an all-around technique for many types of fishing, not only because of its versatility, but also because of its ability to fish at all depths. The angler controls the depth, action and size of a jig. Remember, just because it's called a jig, doesn't mean you have to "jig" it. One of my most effective presentations for weeds is swimming a jig through and over the tops of weeds. Not only will a jig fish over and around weeds, it's the number-one method of fishing in weeds. The technique is easy to do. Simply ease the boat through the weeds with an electric trolling motor or push pole, and drop a jig into each open hole in the weeds. Sounds simple? It is!

Here are a few good tips:
• Use a good pair of polarized sunglasses; the better you see, the better you'll fish.

- Forget about light line; spool up 15 to 20-pound test. Remember, you have to pull the fish out of the weeds once it's hooked.
- Use strong jigs and hooks; you don't want them to straighten out on the hook-set or while pulling a walleye from heavy cover.
- Most importantly, set the hook immediately.
- Remember, fishing jigs in weeds is a calm water technique. If the wind blows, forget it!

Bobbers

Bobbers are great for weed presentations, particularly if you're familiar with a certain patch of weeds. Fish a bobber in the key or high-traffic areas where fish travel such as tips of points, saddles between weed patches, or a mouth of a channel cutting through the weeds.

TROUBLE-SHOOTING TIP

Don't Fish Weeds If It's Windy

When the wind blows, stay out of the weeds, particularly those weeds that rise out above the water's surface. The wind and waves blowing into the weeds create so much movement that the weeds will touch and disturb walleyes. When this happens the walleyes will leave. A good bet for windy days is crankbaits. Cast them 20 to 50 feet away from the weed edge, up wind if possible.

Don't fish bobbers *in* the weeds, the light line and hooks aren't adequate to pull a frisky walleye from heavy cover. Keep bobbers in areas where the fish can be pulled clear of the weeds on the hook-set, and where clear water exists for fighting the fish. Another important point in bobber fishing is a quick hook-set. Don't allow the fish time to pull the bobber into, around and through the weeds which creates a hopeless situation.

Texas Rigging Live Crawlers

Texas rigging nightcrawlers is a technique that can't be beat in scattered weeds. Use a #6 light wire Aberdeen hook behind a 1/32 ounce bullet weight. Hook the nightcrawler through the very tip of the nose, then turn the hook and bury the barb into the body of the nightcrawler. Although the weight is only a 1/32 ounce, when added to the weight of the nightcrawler it's very castable. Cast this rig around, through, or even into the heaviest weeds; it returns absolutely weedless. Retrieve it by slowly pulling the rod tip back and then forward, taking up the slack. If any resistance is felt, stop the action and hold the rod as still as possible to detect any movements. A walleye may be slowly swimming off with the rig. If a hit is recognized, drop the rod tip and allow the fish to swim off with the bait. Give him a few seconds then take up the slack and set the hook.

Jerry Anderson, a 20 year veteran guide on Mille Lacs Lake, understand finicky fish and finesse fishing.

208 WALLEYE TROUBLE-SHOOTING

In-Fisherman Photo

WHY SHOULD YOU FISH THE WINDY SIDE?

What does wind have to do with walleyes? Do walleyes even know that the wind is blowing? Do we need a "walleye chop?" These questions will probably never be answered exactly, but we do learn more and more every year about walleye behavior.

One of the reasons wind makes walleye fishing more effective is simply because of the increased options it adds for presenting your baits. This up and down motion of the waves gives action to the rods in holders, allowing walleye fishermen to use multiple rods. A rod holder is a perfect presentation when waves are rocking the boat. With a wide spread of rods, a wide area of water can be covered on a drift.

Wind permits access to shallow fish without scaring them. Wind creates dirty water, and the walleyes can't see your boat. Wind also allows us to fish closer to the fish because waves camouflage pressure changes caused by the water displacement of our boats.

Water displacement from the boat hull is very important and often overlooked. Walleyes don't necessarily have to see to know what's going on around them. He relates differently to his environment than we do. As humans we expect fish to see things as we see them, hear and feel things as we do and act like we act. But that's not the case, walleyes have a unique major sensory organ, its called a lateral line.

The lateral line works like a big ear. It picks up vibrations, it feels water displacement and can act as a huge "eye" to help the fish "see" when water clarity is reduced to zero. When you troll across a walleye, the hull of the boat will displace an enormous amount of water.

As your boat moves water, a chain reaction is set up as pressure waves continue to move out from the source. This movement is picked up by the walleye's lateral line. Although the walleyes lateral line doesn't recognize or identify the hull displacement as an angler, he does recognize it as this: "Here comes something about 18 feet long, and that's something big enough to eat me!"

A *"good walleye chop!"* In-Fisherman Photo

QUESTION 49   **WHY SHOULD YOU FISH THE WINDY SIDE?**

This may not be an exact quote of the walleye's reaction, but we do know that his senses alert him to change quickly from the offensive to the defensive. You'll find that it's a tough bite if the fish are on the defense.

The lateral line is located along the fish's side. It's the red streak that runs down the fillet. Through a microscope, it looks like tens of thousands of tiny hairs. The hairs lie right under a row of scales which are hollow, filled with a mucus, and transfer water pressure changes to the brain. This is how fish relate to their environment. The lateral line is so sensitive that a fish can feel the smallest of movements.

How sensitive is this sense of "hearing or feeling"? Researcher Joe Lindel says, "With this organ, fish can readily distinguish one baitfish species from another. As a minnow swims by, it gives off unique underwater vibrations that makes it identifiable. Every aquatic creature has its own 'signature,' much like humans have a distinctive set of fingerprints."

Young fish don't have a well-developed lateral line like they will later in life. If you look at a fry (a small, young-of-the-year fish that's just out of the egg), it's no more than an eye with an attached tail and a belly. The eye is the first thing that develops on a little fish which is key to the fish's movement. It's his whole defense. The lateral line hasn't fully developed; therefore, he can't pick up on water displacements and pressure changes. His defensive eye can detect any type of movement, and the fish reacts instantly.

For example, observe minnows slowly finning in an aquarium. They're fairly stationary, but if you wave your hand over them, they scatter. Movement terrorizes small fish. Even leaves blowing off a tree or birds flying overhead will cause them to dart away. That's why in clear water conditions, small fish will see the predator walleye long before the walleye can strike.

When the wind blows, a dramatic change occurs in the world of the young-of-the-year fish. The waves start

212 WALLEYE TROUBLE-SHOOTING

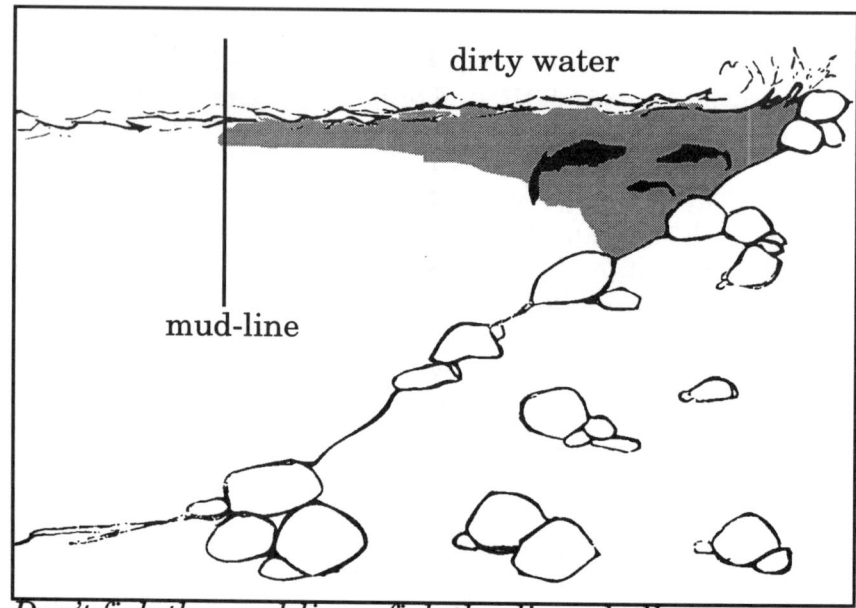

Don't fish the mud-lines, fish the dirty shallow water.

rolling ashore, stirring up the water. This dirty water with suspended solid particles reduces visibility. Walleyes, reacting as if hearing the dinner bell, move into this muddy water to feed, using their lateral lines as eyes. Remember, nothing has X-ray vision. If you can only see three inches into the dirty water, that's all anything else can see.

The small fish act as if they're more comfortable in the dirty water. They can't see movement, which eliminates their defensive shield. They're off-guard and also actively feeding on the suspended particles. The wall-

TROUBLE-SHOOTING TIP
Other Mud-Lines

Although we associate mud-lines with wind, other events such as boat waves, rain, or run off, also create areas of dirty water that will hold fish. Look for them and recognize them, and by all means don't pass them up.

eyes slide into this dirty water along with the big waves. They detect the signature of the minnow's water displacement, ease within a few inches, flare their gills and suck in a volume of water surrounding the baitfish. This draws the water in through their open mouth, filters the flow through their gill rakers, and traps the unsuspecting baitfish in their mouths. Neither fish ever sees the other one! It's easy to understand why dirty water, wind, and big waves act like a dinner bell for walleyes.

Wind can also create new structures in shallow water. These are called mud-lines. Waves crashing against a shoreline or an exposed point often wash clay into the water creating what we refer to as "mud-lines." This "mud" normally suspends in the top two feet of water. It moves along the point, eventually spreading over a large area like an umbrella.

Phenomenal fishing can occur within the first 20 or 30 minutes of the creation of a mud-line. I watch for this constantly in tournaments. If it's a flat calm day and the wind starts to blow, I go immediately to the closest point or flat of shallow water where I believe fish may be holding. When a new mud-line is created, there's an immediate movement of fish into the shallow water. What happens on this early movement into shallow water is a "feeding binge." It becomes a walleye feast because the eating is so easy. When full the fish move back into their comfort zones until they are hungry again.

A few days of the wind blowing into the same areas will support a mud-line that does hold fish, but it can't compare to the frantic action during the first 20 minutes of its creation. I've won several tournaments by fishing the wind. In the South Dakota Governor's Cup in 1987, Bob Propst, Sr., and I led the tournament the first day by just a few ounces. We knew we had a shot to win because the forecast on the second day called for calm winds in the morning and a strong wind by noon.

We motored over the flat surface to the same area

where we had caught fish the first day. By mid-afternoon we had only boated three fish and were beginning to wonder if that wind was ever going to blow. Then looking to the west, Bob remarked about the black, dusty haze on the horizon. A big wind was coming! Within a few minutes the wind hit the opposite side of the reservoir. With the forecast calling for 50 mile per hour winds, the other boats immediately headed for the landing 20 miles away. Bob and I pulled our lines in also, but we aimed for a huge school of fish we knew was in front of the tournament weigh-in site. These fish had been off-bite earlier because of the calm conditions. By the time we arrived at the launch, the waves had reached six to eight feet in height. Most of the other anglers were calling it a day and weighing in their fish.

Bob and I agreed to try one pass on the long point in view of all the other contestants. In one pass, we caught seven fish in an area two hundred feet long. They all came within 15 minutes. We struggled up wind to make one more pass. We now needed only two more fish to complete our limit. When we hit six feet of water, all four rods hooked fish. We kept two for a tournament limit and a great win right in front of everybody! Who could have asked for more?

There's a basic commandment in walleye fishing which says: "Fish the wind." If there's no wind, be prepared for a long day.

TROUBLE-SHOOTING TIP
Watch For Wind Changes

You don't need a switch from flat calm to a 60 mile per hour wind for fishing to improve. Even a wind direction change can do it. For example, if you have a south wind for two days, and all of a sudden it changes 180 degrees, the sheltered areas that had no waves will now become "hot." Watch the wind and be prepared to take advantage of it. If you want to catch a phenomenal number of fish, the wind gives you your best chance.

WHAT DO YOU DO ABOUT TOO MUCH BOAT PRESSURE?

Unfortunatly for walleye fishing, boat pressure is a common problem that's not going away. It's not unusual to see several boats tightly working a small school of walleyes. What is unusual is that each angler will say that he was there first. Forget about who was there first. You have two very clear choices - take it or leave it!

If frustration has set in and you choose to leave, make certain to learn all about the area you're leaving. Take notes on the exact depth of the active fish, along with the successful techniques and colors used. Pay attention to wind direction and water clarity as well as the overall structure, shape, and make of the bottom. All this information can be gathered from the surrounding boats.

Where there's fish - there's boats   In-Fisherman Photo

Now it's only a matter of taking this information and applying it to another part of the lake where you will be alone until you net that first fish.

Should you choose to stay and elbow your way through the boat pressure, pay close attention to the exact spot where fish are caught by you or others. The fish may be in such a tight school that, if missed by a few feet, you're out of luck. Check the direction of bait presentation. Sometimes the smallest observations can make all the difference.

Perhaps you wish to stay, but don't feel like playing an aggressive game of "bumper boats." Here are some options that have produced fish for me. Generally these tightly schooled fish are fairly deep and not aggressively seeking food. They're in a comfort zone (an area chosen because of it's depth, light, water temperature or structure). When these fish decide it's time to eat, they'll leave the comfort zone and move to the food. Many times this movement is to shallow water. Check it out. With heavy boat pressure, never pass up the opportunity to slip between the boats and the shore to fish the shallow water. This could be where the real action is located.

Another option is considering suspended fish. If the boat pressure becomes too much, the fish may move off the structure while holding close to the comfort zone. They maintain their depth and move out over deeper water, sometimes as far as 100 feet off the structure and are prime candidates for trolling crankbaits. Simply choose a lure that hits the same depth as the fish were on the structure and troll around the outside of the boat pack over that deeper water. The results may be surprising, and your success will have the other anglers scratching their heads!